700 Challenging Questions for

Now You Know!

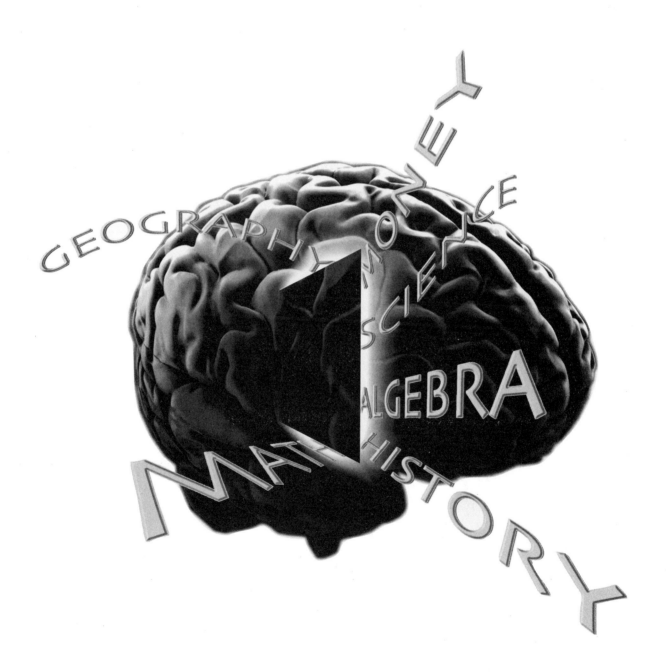

Edward Zaccaro

Ed lives outside of Dubuque, Iowa, with his wife Sara. He has been involved in various areas of education since graduating from Oberlin College in 1974. Ed holds a Masters degree in gifted education from the University of Northern Iowa and has presented at state and national conferences in the areas of mathematics and gifted education.

Layout and design by Blue Room Productions

Copyright ©2012 Edward Zaccaro

All rights reserved. No part of this book may be reproduced or transmitted in any form, including photo-copying, except as may be expressly permitted by the Copyright Act of 1976.

Requests for permission should be addressed to:

Hickory Grove Press
3151 Treeco Lane
Bellevue, Iowa 52031

E-mail: challengemath@aol.com
www.challengemath.com

Teachers and parents may copy for their students. We ask that you be fair and reasonable. Thank you. Photocopying or other means of reproduction of this book or parts of this book for an entire school system is strictly forbidden.

Library of Congress Control Number: 2012906549

ISBN 10: 0985472502

ISBN 13: 978-0-9854725-0-4

Books by Edward Zaccaro

- *Primary Grade Challenge Math*

- *Challenge Math for the Elementary and Middle School Student*

- *Real World Algebra*

- *The Ten Things All Future Mathematicians and Scientists Must Know (But are Rarely Taught)*

- *Becoming a Problem Solving Genius*

- *25 Real Life Math Investigations That Will Astound Teachers and Students*

- *Scammed by Statistics*
  How We are Lied to, Cheated and Manipulated by Statistics

- *Now You Know   Volume 1*

- *Now You Know   Volume 2*

This book is dedicated to my wife Sara, my children Luke, Rachel, and Daniel and their spouses Laura, Jon, and Alicia who all had to endure hundreds of random questions that were asked at all hours of the day and night as **Now You Know** *was being developed. My sincere apologies and appreciation.*

Introduction

This book contains 700 questions that are designed for middle school students, high school students and adults. Some of the questions are meant to just be fun, while others are meant to give the reader a better understanding of math, money, science, geography, history and algebra.

Look at the following science question from Challenge 30:

The animal responsible for the most human deaths worldwide is the _____.

Ⓐ mosquito   Ⓑ hippo   Ⓒ deer   Ⓓ bee

I have found that most children will answer "hippo" while adults will almost always give the correct answer of mosquito. The reason, of course, is that most adults have more of an understanding of the world. Children typically don't view mosquitoes as anything more than a nuisance and are unaware that malaria has killed millions of people worldwide. My hope is that questions like this one will prompt students and adults to do further research and in the process, gain a better understanding of the world.

Several questions from the money section of each challenge are meant to help develop financial literacy. Look at the money question from Challenge 23:

If you have a student loan of $250,000 at 8% interest, how much will you pay each month for the 20 years it takes to pay off the loan?

Ⓐ $600   Ⓑ $1100   Ⓒ $2100   Ⓓ $4500

The student or adult is not expected to be able to "figure out" the answer to this question. The intent of the question is to help develop a rough idea of what interest rates, loans, and debt mean in the real world.
(A part of this understanding is developing the knowledge of how to use an internet mortgage calculator.)

Once a student develops financial literacy, he or she will know that this kind of debt means payments of approximately 2000 dollars each month for 20 years ---- a crushing debt for most college graduates!

As in the above example, there are many other questions, (particularly those involving size, weight, speed, temperature, and dates) where students are not expected to know the exact answer. The purpose of these questions is for the student to acquire a general sense of a time period, or how large or small something is. For example, one question concerns the dates of the Civil War. The question asks for one year the Civil War was fought, not the exact beginning and ending. It is not as important for a student to know that the Civil War was fought from 1861-1865 as it is that he or she know it was fought in the mid-1800's and not the early 1900's.

The intent of **Now You Know** is to help students and adults learn to think deeply and with insight; see the magic and wonders of mathematics, science, geography, and history; and understand and appreciate their place in the world.

All attempts were made to verify the accuracy of all answers, however, some differences of opinion did exist in the research for some of the answers. We welcome feedback as more research becomes available.

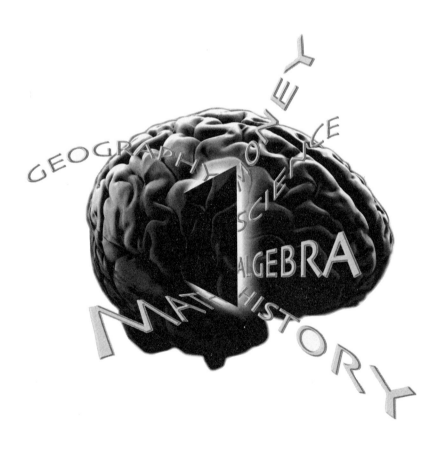

Instructions

 Math

 Money

 Science

 Geography

 History and Government

 Language of Algebra

 Facts and Factoids

Score: ___ / 7

Challenge 1

 In the sequence 1, 4, 9, 16, 25, the 6th number is 36. What is the 20th number?

 A charge of .01 dollars per minute is how many times more expensive than .01 cents per minute?

 The smallest bone found in the human body is located in the middle ear. How long is it?

Ⓐ 1/10 of an inch   Ⓑ 1/2 inch   Ⓒ 1 inch   Ⓓ 1.5 inches

 What is the name of the world's smallest country? (Land mass)

Ⓐ Monaco   Ⓑ Nauru   Ⓒ Liechtenstein   Ⓓ Vatican City

 Name one of the five years the Civil War was fought.

 The value of *n* quarters expressed as cents is:

 The first heart transplant was performed in 1967. How long did the patient live?

Ⓐ 18 hours   Ⓑ 18 days   Ⓒ 18 months   Ⓓ 18 years

Score: ___ / 7

Challenge 2

10^{10} is how many times larger than 10^6?
Ⓐ 10,000 times   Ⓑ 1000 times   Ⓒ 100 times   Ⓓ 4 times

One million dollars is to one trillion dollars as one dollar is to:
Ⓐ $100   Ⓑ $1000   Ⓒ $10,000   Ⓓ $1,000,000

How many times does a heart beat in an average life?
Ⓐ 2,500,000   Ⓑ 250,000,000
Ⓒ 2,500,000,000   Ⓓ 25,000,000,000

The 2011 Tohoku earthquake off the eastern coast of Japan caused a tsunami at the Fukushima power plant with waves as high as:
Ⓐ 45 feet   Ⓑ 80 feet   Ⓒ 130 feet   Ⓓ 300 feet

When was the airplane invented?
Ⓐ 1889   Ⓑ 1900   Ⓒ 1903   Ⓓ 1911

Mary is 5 inches taller than Steve.
If Steve is n inches tall, how tall is Mary?

The weight of a teaspoon of neutron star on earth is closest to the weight of:
Ⓐ One car   Ⓑ 100 cars   Ⓒ 1000 cars   Ⓓ 500,000,000 cars

Score: ___ / 7

Now You Know   13

Challenge 3

What is the probability of rolling 2 of a kind when two dice are rolled?
- Ⓐ 1/6
- Ⓑ 1/36
- Ⓒ 1/18
- Ⓓ 1/3

What did a gallon of milk cost in 1970?
- Ⓐ 25 cents
- Ⓑ $1.15
- Ⓒ $1.75
- Ⓓ $2.25

It takes sound approximately:
- Ⓐ 5 seconds to go one mile
- Ⓑ One second to go one mile
- Ⓒ 1/5 of a second to go one mile
- Ⓓ 1/100 of a second to go one mile

The tallest mountain on earth has an elevation of:
- Ⓐ 1.5 miles
- Ⓑ 5.5 miles
- Ⓒ 6.5 miles
- Ⓓ 9.5 miles

In what time period was the steam locomotive invented?
- Ⓐ 1720-1760
- Ⓑ 1780-1820
- Ⓒ 1820-1860
- Ⓓ 1860-1900

A new building will be *n* feet high.
How many inches will the new building be?

How many ants are there for each person on earth?
- Ⓐ 1000
- Ⓑ 100,000
- Ⓒ 1,000,000
- Ⓓ 1,000,000,000,000

Score: ___ / 7

Challenge 4

If you have 100 feet of fencing, what shape will make a garden with the largest area?

Ⓐ A circle   Ⓑ A rectangle   Ⓒ A square

Ⓓ It doesn't matter, they will all have the same area

If you had 50 billion dollars and spent one million dollars a day, how long would your money last? (Round to nearest year)

Water boils at 212 degrees Fahrenheit at sea level. At what temperature does water boil at the top of Mount Everest?

Ⓐ 154 degrees F   Ⓑ 202 degrees F

Ⓒ 218 degrees F   Ⓓ 264 degrees F

Where does the United States rank in life expectancy? (United Nations data)

Ⓐ 6th   Ⓑ 9th   Ⓒ 16th   Ⓓ 36th

How many people have been president of the United States?

A bike tire does 2400 complete revolutions in a minute. How many revolutions will it do in n seconds?

Ⓐ $n \div 60$ Ⓑ $40n$ Ⓒ $60n \times 2400$ Ⓓ $(n \div 60) \times 2400$

How tall was the tallest female on record?

Ⓐ 7 feet 8.5 inches   Ⓑ 8 feet 7 inches

Ⓒ 8 feet 1.75 inches   Ⓓ 9 feet 1.25 inches

Score: ___ / 7

Challenge 5

Stan has 1,000,000 dollars in base 2.
How much money does he have in base 10?

Ⓐ $64   Ⓑ $1,000,000   Ⓒ $1   Ⓓ $500,000

A United State's dollar converts to $1.25 of Canadian money. What does a dollar of Canadian money convert to in United State's dollars?

Ⓐ $1.00   Ⓑ $1.25   Ⓒ $.75   Ⓓ $.80

The speed of light is how many times faster than the speed of sound?

Ⓐ 10 times   Ⓑ 1000 times
Ⓒ 100,000 times   Ⓓ 1,000,000 times

Water covers _____ of the earth.

Ⓐ 30%   Ⓑ 50%   Ⓒ 70%   Ⓓ 90%

Name one of the five years the first World War was fought.

Sara spent $190 for two presents.
If the first present cost n dollars,
how much did the second one cost?

What was the national debt for the United States on December 12th 2011 at 10:30 Central Time?

Ⓐ $5,107,645,000,000   Ⓑ $10,107,645,000,000
Ⓒ $15,107,645,000,000   Ⓓ $20,107,645,000,000

Score: ___ / 7

Challenge 6

.25% is equal to:
(A) Another way of saying 25% (B) 1/4 (C) 1/40 (D) 1/400

Students graduating from college in 2011 who took out loans to fund their college education had an average student loan debt of:
(A) $8500 (B) $15,500 (C) $25,000 (D) $52,000

A blue whale's weight can be as high as _____ pounds.
(A) 100,000 pounds (B) 300,000 pounds
(C) 1/2 million pounds (D) 100,000 tons

How high would the sea level rise if all of Antarctica's ice sheets melted?
(A) 12 feet (B) 30 feet (C) 100 fee (D) 200 feet

Name the two presidents who were in office during World War II.

My grandfather's age is 5 times my age. My father's age is three times my age and my sister is three years younger than I am. If I am n years old, what is the combined age of all four of us?

The tallest tree ever discovered was:
(A) A 435 foot Australian eucalyptus (B) A 363 foot redwood
(C) A 382 foot pine (D) A 411 foot sequoia

Score: ___ / 7

Challenge 7

If the perimeter of a rectangle is 60 feet and one of the sides is equal to 5 feet, then the area of the rectangle must be:

Ⓐ Impossible to tell from the given information

Ⓑ 125 square feet Ⓒ 250 square feet Ⓓ 300 square feet

Financial experts advise college students to limit their student loans to:

Ⓐ One year's salary for the field they are entering

Ⓑ $50,000 Ⓒ $75,000 Ⓓ $35,000

How many typical viruses would it take to circle a quarter?

Ⓐ 5,000 Ⓑ 50,000 Ⓒ 500,000 Ⓓ 5,000,000

What is the name of the only Great Lake that does not border Canada?

When was World War II fought?

Ⓐ 1928-1933 Ⓑ 1939-1945 Ⓒ 1948-1952 Ⓓ 1951-1956

There are six horses and n ducks on a farm. How many legs are there altogether?

How much gold is in a cubic mile of sea water? (Weight)

Ⓐ Less than an ounce Ⓑ 5 - 10 ounces

Ⓒ 4 - 8 pounds Ⓓ 25 - 100 pounds

Score: ___ / 7

Challenge 8

How long would it take light to travel around the equator of the earth?

- Ⓐ 1/100 of a second
- Ⓑ 1/7 of a second
- Ⓒ 1.4 seconds
- Ⓓ 7 seconds

A home mortgage for a $100,000 loan at an interest rate of 3% would call for a monthly payment of $421.60. If the interest rate was 14%, what would the monthly payment be?

- Ⓐ $686.87
- Ⓑ $886.87
- Ⓒ $1184.87
- Ⓓ Stay the same

The lowest possible temperature expressed in Fahrenheit is:

- Ⓐ -123°F
- Ⓑ -459.67°F
- Ⓒ -1240°F
- Ⓓ No lowest temperature

What percent of the world's fresh water is held in the ice of Antarctica?

- Ⓐ 99%
- Ⓑ 70%
- Ⓒ 25%
- Ⓓ 10%

Name two of the three main countries that the United States was at war with during World War II.

How many millimeters are in *n* meters?

How many people die worldwide each year of smoking related causes?

- Ⓐ 975,000
- Ⓑ 1.2 million
- Ⓒ 5 million
- Ⓓ 65.5 million

Score: ___ / 7

Challenge 9

The circumference of a circle divided by the radius is equal to:

Ⓐ π   Ⓑ 2π   Ⓒ Depends on the size of the circle   Ⓓ πr²

The current national debt (2011) is over 15 trillion dollars.
What was the national debt in 1970?

Ⓐ 381 billion dollars   Ⓑ 2.2 trillion dollars
Ⓒ 4 trillion dollars   Ⓓ 6.3 trillion dollars

What is closest in size to a blue whale's heart?

Ⓐ Beach ball   Ⓑ Washing machine   Ⓒ Walnut   Ⓓ Car

Where does the United States rank in
the list of most populated countries?

Ⓐ 3rd   Ⓑ 5th   Ⓒ 7th   Ⓓ 8th

The Declaration of Independence was signed in 1776. In what year did
George Washington take office as president of the United States?

Ⓐ 1776   Ⓑ 1778   Ⓒ 1780   Ⓓ 1789

How many hours are there in n seconds?

A liter of water weighs:

Ⓐ Approximately 5 pounds   Ⓑ Exactly 1 pound
Ⓒ Exactly 1 kilogram   Ⓓ Approximately 3 pounds

Score: ___ / 7

Challenge 10

A meter is to a nanometer as the earth is to:
Ⓐ Medium size grain of sand Ⓑ Marble Ⓒ Moon Ⓓ Sun

A gallon of gas cost _____ in 1970.
Ⓐ 36 cents Ⓑ 75 cents Ⓒ $1.25 Ⓓ $1.80

How far away is the closest star to earth? (excluding our sun)
Ⓐ 4.2 light years Ⓑ 84.5 light years Ⓒ 964 light years
Ⓓ Over a thousand light years

The longest river in the world is:
Ⓐ The Nile Ⓑ The Amazon Ⓒ The Yangtze
Ⓓ The Mississippi - Missouri - Red Rock system

How many Supreme Court justices are there?

$x=y^2$
What is the sum of five consecutive numbers?
(The smallest is n)

A normal birth weight is 7-8 pounds. In 2004, the world's tiniest baby was born. How much did she weigh at birth? (She is healthy today.)
Ⓐ 9.2 ounces Ⓑ 1.6 pounds Ⓒ 2.1 pounds Ⓓ 2.7 pounds

Score: ___ / 7

Challenge 11

A speed of 60 miles per hour is the same as _____ kilometers per hour.

What was the average price of a new home in 1960?

Ⓐ $12,700   Ⓑ $24,500   Ⓒ $48,500   Ⓓ $62,500

The fastest land animal is the cheetah (65 mph). The slowest land animal is the three-toed sloth. What is the top speed of the three-toed sloth?

Ⓐ .7 miles per hour   Ⓑ .15 miles per hour

Ⓒ 1.2 miles per hour   Ⓓ 1.6 miles per hour

There are only two states that have not had the temperature reach 100° F. Alaska is one, what is the other state?

What are the three branches of government in the United States?

What is the sum of five consecutive even numbers?
(The smallest is *n*)

On average, how many lightning bolts hit the earth each second?

Ⓐ 100   Ⓑ 50   Ⓒ 12   Ⓓ .8

Score: ___ / 7

Challenge 12

What is the next number?
0, 1, 1, 2, 3, 5, 8, 13, 21, 34, 55, ?

A book that cost $80 on Monday is discounted 50% on Tuesday, another 50% on Wednesday and so forth (an additional 50% each day). What will the cost of the book be on Sunday?

The loudest animal is the blue whale. Keeping in mind that a whisper is 30 decibels and a jet engine 140 decibels, how many decibels are the sounds of a blue whale?

Ⓐ 80 decibels   Ⓑ 100 decibels   Ⓒ 185 decibels   Ⓓ 28 decibels

The amount of ice in the Antarctic is what fraction of the amount of water in the Atlantic?

Ⓐ 1/100   Ⓑ 1/10   Ⓒ 1/2   Ⓓ They are the same

In what year was the attack by the Japanese on Pearl Harbor?

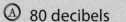

If the circumference of a circle is n, what is the diameter?

How many pounds of food does the average person eat in a lifetime?

Ⓐ 5000 pounds   Ⓑ 25,000 pounds
Ⓒ 60,000 pounds   Ⓓ 150,000 pounds

Score: ___ / 7

Challenge 13

If five barrels each have five cats,
who each have five kittens,
how many total legs are there?

The price of a gallon of milk increased from $8 to $10.
What was the percent of increase?

The smallest rodent is the pigmy jerboa which weighs approximately 1/4 of an ounce. The largest rodent is a capybara. It can weigh as much as_____.

Ⓐ 5 pounds   Ⓑ 50 pounds   Ⓒ 100 pounds   Ⓓ 150 pounds

What country is closest to the United States?
(Not including Canada and Mexico)

Ⓐ Russia   Ⓑ Cuba   Ⓒ Haiti   Ⓓ Bermuda

Who were the presidents during the Civil War,
World War I, and the beginning of the Korean War?

The width of a rectangle is called *n*.
If the length of a rectangle is 8 times the width, what is the perimeter?

For every person who is killed by a shark,
_____ sharks are killed by humans.

Ⓐ 1000   Ⓑ 10,000   Ⓒ 5-10 million   Ⓓ 100 - 200 million

Score: ___ / 7

Challenge 14

Rat A swam across the middle of a lake with a one mile diameter. Rat B walked around the lake to the other side to meet Rat A. How much farther did Rat B travel?

A person who has a net worth of 50 billion dollars gave one million dollars to charity. How much must a person who has a net worth of $1000 give to charity to give away the same fraction of his wealth as the billionaire?

Ⓐ 2 cents   Ⓑ $2   Ⓒ $20   Ⓓ $200

Galapagos tortoises can weigh as much as 500 pounds. What is their life span?

Ⓐ 72 years   Ⓑ 150 years   Ⓒ 95 years   Ⓓ 250 years

There is enough salt in all five oceans to cover all the continents to a depth of nearly _____ feet.

Ⓐ 5 feet   Ⓑ 50 feet   Ⓒ 500 feet   Ⓓ 5000 feet

The shortest war on record was fought between Zanzibar and England in 1896. Zanzibar surrendered after 38 _____.

Ⓐ Seconds   Ⓑ Minutes   Ⓒ Hours   Ⓓ Days

Bill received a 25% raise in 2011. If his original salary is n, what is his new salary?

How long can human tapeworms grow?

Ⓐ 70 feet   Ⓑ 20 feet   Ⓒ 5 feet   Ⓓ 1.5 feet

Score: ___ / 7

Challenge 15

The amount of time it takes for a spacecraft to travel to Mars is _____ times the amount of time it takes for a spacecraft to travel to the Moon.

- Ⓐ 15
- Ⓑ 45
- Ⓒ 85
- Ⓓ 850

People with an excellent credit rating are often able to acquire car loans with a 0% interest. If their credit rating is poor, they often must pay an interest rate of 16%. A 5-year $24,000 car loan at 0% interest has a monthly payment of $400. What is the monthly payment if the interest rate is 16%?

- Ⓐ $476.85
- Ⓑ $505.42
- Ⓒ $583.63
- Ⓓ $885.22

The fastest flier in the animal kingdom is the peregrine falcon. How fast can it fly?

- Ⓐ 90 miles per hour
- Ⓑ 150 miles per hour
- Ⓒ 185 miles per hour
- Ⓓ 225 miles per hour

What is the northern most state of the lower 48 states?

The Tunguska explosion was a powerful explosion that occurred in Russia in 1908. The explosion is thought to have been caused by an exploding large meteoroid or comet fragment at an altitude of several miles above the earth's surface. The power of the Tunguska explosion is thought to have been:

- Ⓐ As powerful as the atomic bomb dropped on Hiroshima, Japan
- Ⓑ 100 times more powerful than the atomic bomb dropped on Hiroshima, Japan
- Ⓒ 1,000 times more powerful than the atomic bomb dropped on Hiroshima, Japan
- Ⓓ As powerful as 10 seconds of energy produced by the sun

Sales tax in a state is 7%. If the cost of a computer without tax is n dollars, what is the amount of sales tax?

The largest recorded tsunami was caused by a landslide in Lituya Bay, Alaska in 1958. How many feet high was it?

- Ⓐ 80 feet
- Ⓑ 145 feet
- Ⓒ 190 feet
- Ⓓ 1720 feet

Score: ___ / 7

Challenge 16

The first 5 prime numbers are:

Ⓐ 2,3,5,7,11   Ⓑ 2,3,4,5,7   Ⓒ 3,4,5,7,11   Ⓓ 1,2,3,5,7

Bill's 2009 salary of $100,000 was cut by 50% in 2010.
He was then given a 50% raise in 2011. What was his 2011 salary?

Ⓐ $50,000   Ⓑ $75,000   Ⓒ $100,000   Ⓓ $87,500

An African black mamba snake releases enough venom in
one bite to kill _____ humans.

Ⓐ 2   Ⓑ 5   Ⓒ 8   Ⓓ over 10

The largest desert in the world is the Sahara Desert. Its area is:
Ⓐ 1/8 the size of the United States
Ⓑ 1/4 the size of the United States
Ⓒ 1/2 the size of the United States
Ⓓ About the same size as the United States

In what year was the most famous San Francisco Earthquake?

Ⓐ 1896   Ⓑ 1906   Ⓒ 1916   Ⓓ 1926

Sales tax is 5%. A computer is on sale for 30% off the original price.
If the original price is *n*,
what is the new price for the computer including tax?

There are more _____ in United State's households
kept as pets than any other animal.

Ⓐ Cats   Ⓑ Dogs   Ⓒ Fish   Ⓓ Rats, hamsters, and ferrets

Score: ___ / 7

Challenge 17

1.1 in base 2 is equal to what number in base 10?

Ⓐ Same   Ⓑ 4   Ⓒ 1.5   Ⓓ 1.01

When buying a house, a good rule is to keep your monthly mortgage payment, including principal, interest, real estate taxes and homeowner's insurance, under _____ of your gross monthly income.

Ⓐ 18%   Ⓑ 28%   Ⓒ 38%   Ⓓ 48%

If a person weighed 200 pounds at the equator, how much would he weigh at the poles?

Ⓐ Same   Ⓑ 199.9 pounds   Ⓒ 200.1 pounds   Ⓓ 201 pounds

The largest recorded earthquake was the Great Chilean Earthquake of May 22, 1960 with a magnitude of:

Ⓐ 8.9   Ⓑ 9.5   Ⓒ 9.8   Ⓓ 10.0

When did the Titanic sink?

Ⓐ 1896   Ⓑ 1906   Ⓒ 1912   Ⓓ 1918

$x=y^2$

Angle B is 3 times larger than angle A, which we will call n. What is the size of angle C?

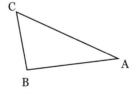

Ants are capable of carrying objects _____ times their body weight.

Ⓐ 5   Ⓑ 15   Ⓒ 35   Ⓓ 50

Score: ___ / 7

Challenge 18

 Sales tax on an item is $22.50. If the tax rate is 7.5%, what was the cost of the item before tax?

 A ballot measure in Arizona called for an 80 cent tax on a pack of cigarettes. The ballot language called for a .80 cent increase. How much money per pack does this ballot language call for?

   Ⓐ 80 cents   Ⓑ 8 cents   Ⓒ .80 dollars   Ⓓ 8/10 of a cent

 Pound for pound, what is the strongest muscle in the body?

   Ⓐ Gluts   Ⓑ Biceps   Ⓒ Tongue   Ⓓ Eyelids

 What is the smallest of the five oceans?

   Ⓐ Arctic   Ⓑ Atlantic   Ⓒ Indian   Ⓓ Southern (Antarctic) Ocean.

 Which president was in office at the time of the Louisiana Purchase?

 There are nickels and dimes in a jar. If there are 20 total coins in the jar and you call the number of nickels n, what is the value of the coins in the jar expressed as cents?

 What was the name of the machine that was used by Nazi Germany for the encryption and decryption of secret messages during World War II?

Score: ___ / 7

Challenge 19

A gold coin with a diameter of 11.6 millimeters is closest in size to which of the following:

 Ⓐ Quarter   Ⓑ Dinner plate   Ⓒ Aspirin   Ⓓ Nickel

The cost of a computer after a 20% discount is $600. What is the regular cost of the computer?

 Ⓐ $750   Ⓑ $800   Ⓒ Not enough information   Ⓓ $900

Even though your brain is only 2% of your total body weight, it requires _____ percent of the oxygen and calories your body needs.

 Ⓐ 20%   Ⓑ 40%   Ⓒ 50%   Ⓓ 80%

What percent of the world's population lives in China?

 Ⓐ 19%   Ⓑ 24%   Ⓒ 29%   Ⓓ 44%

The purchase of Alaska from Russia was called Seward's Folly. Who was the U.S. president at the time of the acquisition?

In a box of change, there are twice as many dimes as nickels and twice as many quarters as dimes. If nickels are called *n*, what is the value of the coins in the box expressed as cents?

How old was the oldest living animal?

 Ⓐ 175 years old   Ⓑ 195 years old

 Ⓒ 245 years old   Ⓓ 405 years old

Score: ___ / 7

Challenge 20

How long would it take sound to travel around the equator of the earth?
- Ⓐ 34.7 seconds
- Ⓑ 34.7 minutes
- Ⓒ 34.7 hours
- Ⓓ 34.7 days

If a 20 year old deposits $100 in a savings account at 2% annual interest, approximately how much money will the $100 have grown to when he is 60 years old?
- Ⓐ $200
- Ⓑ $1000
- Ⓒ $20,000
- Ⓓ $1,000,000

The weight of the world's largest giant sequoia (General Sherman) is _____ pounds.
- Ⓐ 20,000
- Ⓑ 100,000
- Ⓒ 2,500,000
- Ⓓ 100,000,000

What is the northern most, eastern most, and western most state in the United States?
- Ⓐ Alaska, Maine, Alaska
- Ⓑ Alaska, Maine, Hawaii
- Ⓒ Alaska, Alaska, Alaska
- Ⓓ Alaska, Massachusetts, Hawaii

Name the two pairs of father-son presidents.
(The 4th and the 6th as well as the 41st and the 43rd)

Eric is half his father's height. Eric's pet dog is half Eric's height and also twice the height of Eric's pet cat. Eric's hamster is 1/4 the height of the cat. If the hamster is n inches tall, how tall is Eric's dad?

The giant sequoia is the world's most massive living thing. The largest giant sequoia, named General Sherman, has a circumference at the base of _____ feet.
- Ⓐ 5
- Ⓑ 10
- Ⓒ 35
- Ⓓ 100

Score: ___ / 7

Challenge 21

How long does it take light from the sun to reach the earth?

You borrow $500 from a bank for a computer.
If the annual interest rate is 5% and you pay the minimum monthly payment of $15, how long will it take to pay off the loan?

Ⓐ 1 year   Ⓑ 3 years   Ⓒ 5 years   Ⓓ 10 years

How many miles of blood vessels are in the human body?

Ⓐ 10 miles   Ⓑ 600 miles   Ⓒ 60,000 miles   Ⓓ 6,000,000 miles

The name and population of the world's most populous metropolitan area is:

Ⓐ Tokyo with 33,000,000 people
Ⓑ Mexico City with 17,000,000 people
Ⓒ Tokyo with 17,000,000 people
Ⓓ Mexico City with 33,000,000 people

Name 11 of the original 13 colonies:

The perimeter of a rectangle is 7 times the width.
If the width is *n*, what is the length of the rectangle?

A rain drop will always break into smaller drops when it reaches its maximum speed. A rain drop's top speed is:

Ⓐ 18 mph   Ⓑ 28 mph   Ⓒ 38 mph   Ⓓ 48 mph

Score: ___ / 7

Challenge 22

Usain Bolt holds the world record for the 100 meter sprint at 9.58 seconds. How many miles per hour is this speed?

Ⓐ 23.3 miles per hour Ⓑ 28.4 miles per hour
Ⓒ 32.3 miles per hour Ⓓ 38.4 miles per hour

If a 20 year old deposits $100 in a savings account at 12% annual interest, approximately how much money will the $100 have grown to when he is 60 years old?

Ⓐ $1200   Ⓑ $12,000   Ⓒ $120,000   Ⓓ $12,000,000

How far is Mars from the Sun?

Ⓐ 80,000,000 miles   Ⓑ 93,000,000 miles
Ⓒ 130,000,000 miles Ⓓ 200,000,000 miles

It has recently been discovered that Florida and the Hudson Bay are getting _____ closer every year. (Distance)

Ⓐ 2/3 of a millimeter   Ⓑ 2.5 inches
Ⓒ 2.5 feet   Ⓓ 25 nanometers

What amendment gave women the right to vote?

A pie is divided into n equal pieces and 6 are then eaten. What fraction of the pie is left?

Ⓐ 2   Ⓑ $1/n$ Ⓒ $n/6$ Ⓓ $(n-6) \div n$

A typical American car can travel 25 miles per gallon of gas. How many miles will a 747 jet travel for each gallon of jet fuel?

Ⓐ 1/100 of a mile   Ⓑ 1/20 of a mile
Ⓒ 1/5 of a mile   Ⓓ Just under a mile

Score: ___ / 7

Challenge 23

A googol is defined as a one followed by how many zeros?
- Ⓐ 100
- Ⓑ 1000
- Ⓒ 1,000,000
- Ⓓ 10 to the 100th power

If you have a student loan of $250,000 at 8% interest, how much will you pay each month for the 20 years it takes to pay off the loan?
- Ⓐ $600
- Ⓑ $1100
- Ⓒ $2100
- Ⓓ $4500

How many electrons are in an atom of uranium?
- Ⓐ 72
- Ⓑ 92
- Ⓒ 98
- Ⓓ 112

What is the name of the world's largest country? (Land mass)
- Ⓐ China
- Ⓑ Russia
- Ⓒ Canada
- Ⓓ Brazil

The amendment that gave women the right to vote was ratified in:
- Ⓐ 1820
- Ⓑ 1870
- Ⓒ 1920
- Ⓓ 1950

Alicia traveled n hours at 60 miles per hour. How many miles has she traveled?

How many people are killed each year in the United States by lightning, sharks, bees and dogs?
- Ⓐ Lightning 58; Sharks .5; Bees 50; Dogs 30
- Ⓑ Lightning 8; Sharks .3; Bees 89; Dogs 18
- Ⓒ Lightning 20; Sharks .1; Bees 60; Dogs 9
- Ⓓ Lightning 3; Sharks 3; Bees 110; Dogs 13

Score: ___ / 7

Challenge 24

$8^0 + 8^0 + 1^0$ is equal to:

Ⓐ 0　　Ⓑ 16　　Ⓒ 1　　Ⓓ 3

If you have a student loan of $250,000 at 3% interest, how much will you pay each month for the 20 years it takes to pay off the loan?

Ⓐ $400　　Ⓑ $800　　Ⓒ $2200　　Ⓓ $1400

What is the temperature at the center of the sun?
Ⓐ 27,000 degrees Fahrenheit
Ⓑ 270,000 degrees Fahrenheit
Ⓒ 27,000,000 degrees Fahrenheit
Ⓓ 27,000,000,000 degrees Fahrenheit

The longest name for a village is in Wales. How many letters does it have?

Ⓐ 59 letters　　Ⓑ 165 letters　　Ⓒ 283 letters　　Ⓓ 437 letters

How long was the Lewis and Clark expedition?

Ⓐ 8 months　　Ⓑ 11 months
Ⓒ 1 year 11 months　　Ⓓ 2 years 4 months

Natalie is going on a 900 mile trip. So far, she has traveled n hours at 60 miles per hour. How many miles of her trip does she have remaining?

What percent of the world's population used the internet in 2011?

Ⓐ 15%　　Ⓑ 25%　　Ⓒ 40%　　Ⓓ 4%

Score: ___ / 7

Challenge 25

What is the probability of rolling three of the same number when you roll three dice?

  Ⓐ 1/216   Ⓑ 1/36   Ⓒ 1/18   Ⓓ 1/6

"Rent to own" companies usually end up charging consumers _____ the cost of the item.

  Ⓐ $100 more than   Ⓑ 3 to 4 times

  Ⓒ twice   Ⓓ 50% more than

The distance from the Earth to Mars, when they are at their closest, is _____ times the distance from the Earth to the Moon at their closest.

  Ⓐ 85   Ⓑ 150   Ⓒ 315   Ⓓ 885

Put these places in order from west to east: Anchorage, Hawaii, Tahiti.

  Ⓐ Anchorage, Hawaii, Tahiti
  Ⓑ Tahiti, Anchorage, Hawaii
  Ⓒ Tahiti, Hawaii, Anchorage
  Ⓓ Hawaii, Anchorage, Tahiti

The treaty between Great Britain and the United States that gave recognition to the existence of the United States was:

  Ⓐ Treaty of Paris   Ⓑ Cornwallis Treaty

  Ⓒ Yorktown Treaty   Ⓓ Treaty of Independence

Each week Daniel is paid $8.50 per hour plus a bonus of $50. How much did he earn in a week where he worked n hours?

  Ⓐ $8.50n + $50   Ⓑ $390

  Ⓒ Not enough information   Ⓓ $n + $50

How long can a sperm whale hold its breath?

  Ⓐ 2 hours   Ⓑ 50 minutes   Ⓒ 8-9 hours   Ⓓ 20-30 minutes

Score: ___ / 7

Challenge 26

What is the next number in the following list of numbers? 1, 8, 27, 64, ?
- Ⓐ 99
- Ⓑ 114
- Ⓒ 125
- Ⓓ 128

In what year was the price of a first class stamp 6 cents?
- Ⓐ 1940
- Ⓑ 1950
- Ⓒ 1960
- Ⓓ 1970

How much would a 200 pound person weigh on the moon?
- Ⓐ 33 pounds
- Ⓑ 45 pounds
- Ⓒ 88 pounds
- Ⓓ Would not change

The country with the longest life expectancy for a female is Japan at _____ years old. (United Nations data)
- Ⓐ 79.8
- Ⓑ 80.4
- Ⓒ 86.1
- Ⓓ 90.2

What was the primary event/events which led to the United States entering World War I?

This bread is n minutes old. How old is the bread expressed in days?
- Ⓐ $60n \times 24$
- Ⓑ Not enough information
- Ⓒ $n/24$
- Ⓓ $n/1440$

Which state had the most deaths caused by lightning from 2001-2010?

Score: __ / 7

Challenge 27

How many cubic inches are in a cubic foot?

Ⓐ 12   Ⓑ 144   Ⓒ 1728   Ⓓ 20,736

Total outstanding student loan debt for the United States in 2011 was:

Ⓐ 950 billion dollars   Ⓑ 2.3 trillion dollars
Ⓒ 10.3 trillion dollars   Ⓓ 28.5 trillion dollars

The diameter of the sun is approximately
how many times larger than the diameter of the earth?

Ⓐ 100   Ⓑ 1000   Ⓒ 10,000   Ⓓ 100,000

Hawaii is moving toward Japan at a rate of _____ per year.

Ⓐ 4 millimeters   Ⓑ 4 inches   Ⓒ 4 feet   Ⓓ 4 meters

What was the name of the first man-made satellite?

If you can throw a baseball n feet,
how many miles can you throw a baseball?

Robert Wadlow is considered to be the tallest person in history.
How tall was he?

Ⓐ 8 feet 11.1 inches   Ⓑ 9 feet 2.5 inches
Ⓒ 9 feet 8.3 inches   Ⓓ 10 feet 1.1 inches

Score: ___ / 7

Challenge 28

In a box containing red and blue marbles, 30 marbles are picked at random and the result is 12 red and 18 blue marbles. After the 30 marbles are replaced, the box contains a total of 1000 marbles. How many red marbles would you estimate are in the box?

  Ⓐ 250   Ⓑ 300   Ⓒ 400   Ⓓ 600

If you have a credit card balance of $50,000 at 34.9% interest, how much will you pay each month for the 5 years it takes to pay off the loan?

  Ⓐ $900   Ⓑ $1200   Ⓒ $1500   Ⓓ $1800

Approximately how many stars are in the universe?

  Ⓐ 100 trillion   Ⓑ 10^{23} Ⓒ 10^{87} Ⓓ $10^{1,000,000,000}$

The longest bridge in the United States is the Lake Pontchartrain Causeway. How long is it?

  Ⓐ 5.8 miles   Ⓑ 8.9 miles   Ⓒ 23.9 miles   Ⓓ 40.9 miles

Which president started a relationship with China?

  Ⓐ Kennedy   Ⓑ Nixon   Ⓒ Eisenhower   Ⓓ Johnson

If a farm has n cows, 10 pigs and one duck, how many legs are on the farm?

What is the probability of being bitten by a dog in the United States in a given year?

  Ⓐ 1/50   Ⓑ 1/500   Ⓒ 1/5000

Ⓓ About the same probability as being struck by lightning

Score: ___ / 7

Challenge 29

What is the lowest common denominator for
1/2, 1/3, 1/4, 1/5, and 1/6?

 Ⓐ 30 Ⓑ 60 Ⓒ 90 Ⓓ None of the above

What does it cost to raise a medium-size dog to the age of eleven?

 Ⓐ $1840 Ⓑ $6440 Ⓒ $10,400 Ⓓ $16,400

How hot is lightning?

 Ⓐ As hot as the surface of the sun
 Ⓑ As hot as the center of the sun
 Ⓒ 6 times hotter than the surface of the sun
 Ⓓ Twice as hot as the center of the sun

The wettest place on earth is
Mawsynram, Meghalaya (India) with _____ of rainfall each year.

 Ⓐ 285 inches Ⓑ 467 inches Ⓒ 580 inches Ⓓ almost 72 feet

The _____ Doctrine said that European countries
should not try to gain influence in the Western Hemisphere.

Solve for n : $1/2n - 4 = 20$

Pick the true statement about the rate of infant eye blinking.

 Ⓐ Infants blink 5 times more often than adults
 Ⓑ Infants blink 10 times more often than adults
 Ⓒ Infants blink 1 or 2 times each minute
 Ⓓ Infants blink twice as often as adults

Score: ___ / 7

Challenge 30

$6 + 4 \div 2 \times 0 =$

Ⓐ 6   Ⓑ 5   Ⓒ 0   Ⓓ Several answers are possible

What is .50% of $500?

The animal responsible for the most human deaths worldwide is the _____.

Ⓐ mosquito   Ⓑ hippo   Ⓒ deer   Ⓓ bee

The highest waterfall on earth is Angel Falls in Venezuela. How high is it?

Ⓐ 188 feet   Ⓑ 412 feet   Ⓒ 1042 feet   Ⓓ 2648 feet

Which presidents served during the Great Depression?

There are 35 total animals on a farm. If there are only goats and ducks and we call the number of ducks n, how many goats are there?

A cubic foot of water weighs 62.4 pounds. What does a cubic foot of gold weigh?

Ⓐ 1206 pounds   Ⓑ 1580 pounds
Ⓒ A little more than a ton   Ⓓ 32,058 pounds

Score: ___ / 7

Challenge 31

What is closest to the value of pi?
- Ⓐ 3
- Ⓑ 3.14
- Ⓒ The ratio of the circumference of a circle to the diameter
- Ⓓ The area of a circle divided by the circumference

The Dow-Jones Industrial Average is near 12,000 today (2011). What was the lowest level for the Dow-Jones in 1970?
- Ⓐ $225
- Ⓑ $669
- Ⓒ $2125
- Ⓓ $3640

Pterodactyls had wingspans as wide as _____ feet.
- Ⓐ 22 feet
- Ⓑ 28 feet
- Ⓒ 34 feet
- Ⓓ 40 feet

What is the mean income and median income of the 7 billion world population?
- Ⓐ $200 and $800
- Ⓑ $1200 and $4200
- Ⓒ $1700 and $7000
- Ⓓ $8000 and $22,000

The Emancipation Proclamation:
- Ⓐ Freed the slaves
- Ⓑ Gave women the right to vote
- Ⓒ Prohibited the sale of alcohol
- Ⓓ None of the above

The distance around a circular pool is *n* meters. What is the distance in centimeters?

What is the exact length of a day?
(to the nearest second)

Score: ___ / 7

Challenge 32

If you hear thunder 20 seconds after there is a lightning strike, the storm is how many miles away?

Ⓐ 20 miles Ⓑ 10 miles Ⓒ 5 miles Ⓓ 4 miles

In what year was the price of eggs 91 cents?

Ⓐ 1960 Ⓑ 1970 Ⓒ 1980 Ⓓ 1990

How fast does sound travel in water?

Ⓐ 4-5 times faster than air Ⓑ 4-5 times slower than air
Ⓒ 4-5 miles per second Ⓓ Same as air

The coldest temperature recorded on earth was in Vostok, Antarctica. What was the temperature?

Ⓐ -56.6° F Ⓑ -98.6° F Ⓒ -128.6° F Ⓓ -272.6°F

When was the United Nations formed?

Ⓐ After the Korean War Ⓑ After World War II
Ⓒ After World War I Ⓓ After the Civil War

What is the average of five consecutive numbers where the smallest number is n?

How many gallons of jet fuel does a fully loaded 747 use when it travels from Boston to Los Angeles?

Ⓐ 1500 gallons Ⓑ 15,000 gallons
Ⓒ 25,000 gallons Ⓓ 50,000 gallons

Score: ___ / 7

Challenge 33

What is the result when you take
1/2 of 1/25 and then square 1/2 of that answer?

Ⓐ 1/10,000　　Ⓑ 1/500　　Ⓒ 1/2500　　Ⓓ None of the above

How much does it cost to pay for the electricity if a
250-watt incandescent bulb is on for 24 hours and electricity
cost 10 cents per kilowatt hour?

How many grains of sand are there on the earth?

Ⓐ 10^{21}　　Ⓑ 10^{80}　　Ⓒ 10^{2000}　　Ⓓ $10^{3,000,000}$

The hottest temperature recorded on earth was in El Azizia, Libya.
What was the temperature?

Ⓐ 136°F　　Ⓑ 146°F　　Ⓒ 156°F　　Ⓓ 185°F

When was the League of Nations formed?

Ⓐ After the Korean War　　Ⓑ After World War II
Ⓒ After World War I　　Ⓓ After the Civil War

The distance across (diameter) a circular pool is *n* meters.
What is the circumference in decimeters?

Chandra Bahadur Dangi is considered to be the shortest person on record.
How tall is he?

Ⓐ 12.2 inches　　Ⓑ 16.8 inches
Ⓒ 21.5 inches　　Ⓓ 28.2 inches

Score: ___ / 7

Challenge 34

What is the probability of flipping a coin and getting 10 heads in a row?
- Ⓐ Approximately 1 in a million
- Ⓑ Approximately 1 in 1000
- Ⓒ 1 in 512
- Ⓓ 1 in 64

What is .01% of $100?

How long does it take for light to travel from the center of the sun to the surface?
- Ⓐ .5 to .75 seconds
- Ⓑ 10 to 12 seconds
- Ⓒ 100 to 200 years
- Ⓓ 100,000 to 200,000 years

What percent of the world's population lives in the Northern Hemisphere?
- Ⓐ 55%   Ⓑ 65%   Ⓒ 80%   Ⓓ 90%

When was Social Security established?
- Ⓐ 1895   Ⓑ 1915   Ⓒ 1935   Ⓓ 1955

If there are n quarts of water in a bathtub, how many gallons are there in the tub?

What percent of the world's population is male?
- Ⓐ 49.2%   Ⓑ 49.6%   Ⓒ 50.1%   Ⓓ 50.4%

Score: ___ / 7

Challenge 35

A cubic millimeter is what fraction of a cubic meter?
- Ⓐ 1/100
- Ⓑ 1/1,000,000
- Ⓒ 1/1,000,000,000
- Ⓓ 1/1,000,000,000,000

The price of a gallon of milk decreased from $10 to $8. What was the percent of decrease?

How many earths would fit inside the sun?
- Ⓐ 1,300,000
- Ⓑ 130,000
- Ⓒ 13,000
- Ⓓ 1300

Since its formation some 12,000 years ago, how far has Niagara Falls withdrawn upstream?
- Ⓐ 200 feet
- Ⓑ .75 miles
- Ⓒ 3 miles
- Ⓓ 7 miles

When was Medicare established?
- Ⓐ 1915
- Ⓑ 1935
- Ⓒ 1945
- Ⓓ 1965

Jim ate .3475 of n pies. How many pies are left?

How many people in the United States die of smoking related causes each year?
- Ⓐ 38,000
- Ⓑ 438,000
- Ⓒ 1.4 million
- Ⓓ 2.1 million

Score: ___ / 7

Challenge 36

The distance from the earth to the moon is what fraction of the distance of the earth to the sun?
- Ⓐ 1/10
- Ⓑ They are the same distance from the earth
- Ⓒ 1/100
- Ⓓ 1/400

How many billionaires are there in the world?
- Ⓐ 100
- Ⓑ 1000
- Ⓒ 5000
- Ⓓ 10,000

Approximately how many stars are in our galaxy? (Milky Way)
- Ⓐ 2,000,000
- Ⓑ 200,000,000
- Ⓒ 2,000,000,000
- Ⓓ 200,000,000,000

Sea water has a salt content of roughly 3.5%. The Dead Sea has a salt content of ____ percent.
- Ⓐ 10
- Ⓑ 30
- Ⓒ 50
- Ⓓ 90

Which president was known for saying the phrase: "Speak softly, but carry a big stick."?
- Ⓐ Theodore Roosevelt
- Ⓑ Franklin Roosevelt
- Ⓒ Richard Nixon
- Ⓓ Abraham Lincoln

A bat and ball together cost $10. If the bat cost $9 more than the ball, what is the cost of the ball?

What is the median age of the population of the United States?
- Ⓐ 51 years old
- Ⓑ 19 years old
- Ⓒ 12 years old
- Ⓓ 37 years old

Score: ___ / 7

Challenge 37

You are given a penny on December 1st, 2 pennies on the 2nd, 4 pennies on the 3rd, 8 on the 4th, 16 on the 5th and so forth. How much money will you be given on December 31? (Express your answer in dollars.)

What saving's interest rate would be needed to double $100 in 5 years?

    Ⓐ 5%   Ⓑ 9%   Ⓒ 14%   Ⓓ 19%

How fast does the earth spin?

    Ⓐ 60 mph   Ⓑ 500 mph
    Ⓒ 1000 mph   Ⓓ The speed of sound

The world's highest waterfall is how many times higher than Niagara Falls?

    Ⓐ 15 times   Ⓑ 10 times   Ⓒ 5 times   Ⓓ Twice as high

In what year was an atomic bomb dropped on Hiroshima?

    Ⓐ 1943   Ⓑ 1944   Ⓒ 1945   Ⓓ 1946

How many 8 foot sections of fencing are needed for a garden with a length that is 4 times its width? (Call width n)

What is the golden ratio?

    Ⓐ 1.25   Ⓑ 1.41   Ⓒ 1.5   Ⓓ 1.62

Score: ___ / 7

Challenge 38

How many different ways are there to hang four paintings on four hooks?

Ⓐ 12   Ⓑ 24   Ⓒ 36   Ⓓ 48

Which is more expensive,
89 cents a square foot or $5 a square yard?

At what temperature are Fahrenheit and Celsius the same number?

Israel's Dead Sea's surface is _____ feet below sea level.

Ⓐ 122   Ⓑ 368   Ⓒ 892   Ⓓ 1320

The 18th amendment was undone by the 21st amendment.
What was the subject of both amendments?

There are 35 total animals on a farm. If there are only goats and ducks and we call the number of ducks n, how many goats legs are there?

How deep can a sperm whale dive?

Ⓐ 300-500 feet   Ⓑ 5000-10,000 feet
Ⓒ 800-1000 feet   Ⓓ Five times the depth limit of scuba divers

Score: ___ / 7

Challenge 39

One two-digit number is a perfect square and a perfect cube. What is it?

The annual salary for the President of the United States + the annual salary of the Vice-President + the salary of the Chief Justice of the U.S. Supreme Court =

Ⓐ $854,200   Ⓑ $1,058,400   Ⓒ $1,458,200   Ⓓ $1,512,000

What is the temperature on the surface of the sun?

Ⓐ 10,000 degrees Fahrenheit   Ⓑ 100,000 degrees Fahrenheit
Ⓒ 1,000,000 degrees Fahrenheit   Ⓓ 10,000,000 degrees Fahrenheit

How long is the longest river in the world?

Ⓐ 4180 miles   Ⓑ 5450 miles   Ⓒ 6625 miles   Ⓓ 7220 miles

Which amendment states that any person born in the United States is a citizen of the United States?

If it takes n seconds to paint a wall, how many hours does it take to paint the wall?

Ⓐ $60n$ Ⓑ $n \div 60$ Ⓒ $n \div 3600$ Ⓓ Not enough information

How tall was Napoleon?

Ⓐ 5 feet .5 inches   Ⓑ 5 feet 2.5 inches
Ⓒ 5 feet 6.5 inches   Ⓓ 5 feet 11.5 inches

Score: ___ / 7

Challenge 40

A watch with an hour hand and a minute hand gains 16 minutes every day. Every _____ days, this broken watch will show the correct time.

- Ⓐ 30 days
- Ⓑ 45 days
- Ⓒ 90 days
- Ⓓ 365 days

The annual salary for the president of the United States in 1789 was:

- Ⓐ No salary
- Ⓑ $5000
- Ⓒ $25,000
- Ⓓ $75,000

Argentinosaurus is currently thought to have been the biggest dinosaur. What is it estimated to have weighed?

- Ⓐ 50,000 pounds
- Ⓑ 100,000 pounds
- Ⓒ 100 tons
- Ⓓ 500 tons

The deepest part of the ocean is called the Mariana Trench. What is its depth?

- Ⓐ 6.75 miles
- Ⓑ 10.25 miles
- Ⓒ 12.45 miles
- Ⓓ 16.25 miles

"We the people of the United States" is the beginning of:

- Ⓐ Gettysburg Address
- Ⓑ Declaration of Independence
- Ⓒ The pamphlet *Common Sense*
- Ⓓ Constitution

My grandfather's age is 5 times my age. My father's age is three times my age and my sister is three years younger than I am. If I am n years old and the combined age of all four of us is 157, how old am I?

What is Alfred Nobel most famous for inventing?

- Ⓐ X-rays
- Ⓑ Thermometer
- Ⓒ Dynamite
- Ⓓ The concept of a treaty

Score: ___ / 7

Challenge 41

If a laser was bounced off a mirror on the moon, how long would it take for the round trip to the moon and back?

- Ⓐ .15 seconds
- Ⓑ 2.5 seconds
- Ⓒ 3 minutes 20 seconds
- Ⓓ 3 hours 10 minutes

What does FDIC stand for?

All planets rotate in the same direction except one. Which planet is it?

In 2008, hydroelectricity supplied approximately _____ percent of the world's electricity.

- Ⓐ Less than 1%
- Ⓑ 1% - 3%
- Ⓒ 5% - 10%
- Ⓓ 15% - 20%

What happened to Czar Romanov and his family after the Bolshevik Revolution in 1917?

- Ⓐ They were exiled
- Ⓑ They were imprisoned
- Ⓒ They were allowed to live in Russia under house arrest
- Ⓓ They were imprisoned and then executed

Lynn's wage is n dollars per hour plus a bonus of $25 per week. What is Lynn's yearly salary when she works a 40-hour week?

Modern wind turbines usually have 3 blades which can reach speeds (at the tip) of :

- Ⓐ 50 mph
- Ⓑ 100 mph
- Ⓒ 150 mph
- Ⓓ 200 mph

Score: ___ / 7

Challenge 42

 How far will a car travel in 45 seconds if its speed is 60 miles per hour?

 Until 1971, the United States regulated the value of gold. The price of gold was set at _____.

Ⓐ $35 per ounce Ⓑ $85 per ounce
Ⓒ $375 per ounce Ⓓ $575 per ounce

 Humans have 46 chromosomes. One type of ant has the fewest number of chromosomes. How many?

Ⓐ 2 chromosomes Ⓑ 4 chromosomes
Ⓒ 6 chromosomes Ⓓ 12 chromosomes

 The Panama Canal was one of the most difficult engineering projects ever attempted. How many people lost their lives during the building of the Panama Canal (French and American)?

Ⓐ 1000 Ⓑ 5000 Ⓒ 25,000

Ⓓ Miraculously, no one lost their life during the project

 The majority of the Vikings came from three countries. Name two.

 The charge to rent a car is $19.95 per day plus $.12 per mile. What is the cost of renting a car for n days when it is driven t miles?

 In 1997 wind power generated only 0.1% of the world's electricity. What percent of the world's electricity was generated by wind power in 2010?

Ⓐ .5% Ⓑ 1.5% Ⓒ 2.5% Ⓓ 8.5%

Score: ___ / 7

Challenge 43

A coin is flipped three times.
If any of the three flips are heads, you win the game.
What is your probability of winning?

How many 2011 United State's dollars would you need to have the same buying power of one United State's dollar in 1960?

 Ⓐ $3.46 Ⓑ $5.72 Ⓒ $7.46 Ⓓ $12.32

Water boils at 212°F. At what temperature does liquid nitrogen boil?

 Ⓐ -21°F Ⓑ -121°F Ⓒ -221°F Ⓓ -321°F

The Delaware Aqueduct is drilled through solid rock and is the longest tunnel in the world (as of 2010). How long is it?

 Ⓐ 42 miles Ⓑ 85 miles Ⓒ 398 miles Ⓓ 528 miles

Who said the following quote?

"Mr. Gorbachev, tear down this wall."

A cell phone company charges $40 per month plus $.08 per text. What is the monthly bill for someone who makes n texts each month?

Jeanne Calment is thought to be the person to have lived the longest. She was _____ when she died in 1997.

 Ⓐ 118 years old Ⓑ 122 years old
 Ⓒ 128 years old Ⓓ 135 years old

Score: ___ / 7

Challenge 44

The weight of a million dollars worth of pennies (a little over 3.1 grams each) is equivalent to the weight of how many mini-vans?
- Ⓐ 1.5 mini-vans
- Ⓑ 12.5 mini-vans
- Ⓒ 42 mini-vans
- Ⓓ 170 mini-vans

A 2011 dollar has the same buying power as how much money in 1960?
- Ⓐ 13 cents
- Ⓑ 26 cents
- Ⓒ 39 cents
- Ⓓ 52 cents

In what year did a person first see a live cell through a microscope?
- Ⓐ 1224
- Ⓑ 1674
- Ⓒ 1784
- Ⓓ 1848

What percent of volcanic activity takes place in the oceans?
- Ⓐ 20%
- Ⓑ 50%
- Ⓒ 60%
- Ⓓ 80%

Which U.S. president said the following quote?

"A house divided against itself cannot stand."

Ian had 4 more dimes than quarters.
He also has 4 fewer nickels than quarters.
What is the value of his coins if he has *n* quarters?

Airbags in cars sometimes deploy without the car being involved in an accident. What triggers the deployment?
- Ⓐ The car hits a pothole
- Ⓑ The driver slams on the brakes
- Ⓒ A bird hits the front of the car at the sensor
- Ⓓ Very hard rainfall

Score: ___ / 7

Challenge 45

What is 1% of 1% of $100?

A 2011 dollar has the same buying power as how much money in 1914?
Ⓐ 5 cents   Ⓑ 12 cents   Ⓒ 21 cents   Ⓓ 32 cents

In what year was the sound barrier officially broken in a manned aircraft?
Ⓐ 1937   Ⓑ 1947   Ⓒ 1957   Ⓓ 1967

The second largest lake in the world is Lake Superior with an area of 31,820 square miles. The largest lake in the world is the Caspian Sea. It has an area that is _____ times the size of Lake Superior.
Ⓐ 1.5   Ⓑ 2.5   Ⓒ 3.5   Ⓓ 4.5

Which U.S. president said the following quote?

"Ask not what your country can do for you, ask what you can do for your country."

Amy always saves 1/4 of her allowance. If Amy's allowance is *n* dollars per week, what will she have saved in a year?

How many gallons of air does the average person breathe each day?
Ⓐ 30 gallons   Ⓑ 300 gallons
Ⓒ 3000 gallons   Ⓓ 30,000 gallons

Score: ___ / 7

Challenge 46

If a bank pays 3% annual interest, the interest for one day if you deposit $1000 is 8 cents. What is the interest earned for one day if you have one billion dollars in the bank?

Ⓐ $945   Ⓑ $2080   Ⓒ $82,200   Ⓓ $1,000,500

If instead of buying a $6000 laptop from Apple in 1997, you bought Apple stock, your $6000 investment would be worth _____ today.

Ⓐ $50,000   Ⓑ $200,000   Ⓒ $350,000   Ⓓ $3,500,000

What is the reason that a loud noise is heard during the crack of a whip?

What percent of the earth's water is saltwater?

Ⓐ 55%   Ⓑ 67%   Ⓒ 87%   Ⓓ 97%

Which president of the United States said the following quote?

"I am not a crook."

If a kangaroo can hop at a speed of n miles per hour, what is its speed in miles per minute?

Blue whales can communicate with other whales at a distance of _____ miles.

Ⓐ 5 miles   Ⓑ 10 miles   Ⓒ 100 miles   Ⓓ 1000 miles

Score: ___ / 7

Challenge 47

How many liters of water will fit into one cubic meter?
Ⓐ 50 Ⓑ 100 Ⓒ 500 Ⓓ 1000

If an $800 profit is going to be split between three people in a ratio of 5:3:2, what does the person receive who will receive the least amount?

At what speed, in miles per hour, does a plane break the sound barrier? (at sea level)
Ⓐ 460 mph Ⓑ 560 mph Ⓒ 660 mph Ⓓ 760 mph

What percent of the earth's freshwater is frozen?
Ⓐ 35% Ⓑ 65% Ⓒ 95% Ⓓ 99%

Which president of the United States said the following quote? "In the councils of government, we must guard against the acquisition of unwarranted influence, whether sought or unsought, by the military-industrial complex. The potential for the disastrous rise of misplaced power exists and will persist."

If a kangaroo can hop at a speed of n miles per hour, what is its speed in miles per second?

What percent of an iceberg is below the surface of the water?
Ⓐ 10% Ⓑ 50% Ⓒ 90% Ⓓ 99%

Score: ___ / 7

Challenge 48

 What is the surface area of a cubic yard expressed in square feet?

 $30,000 has been charged on a credit card with an annual interest rate of 20%. If only the interest is paid each month, what is the monthly payment?

ⓐ $100 ⓑ $300 ⓒ $500 ⓓ $700

 Galapagos tortoises have one of the longest life spans of animals. Mayflies have one of the shortest life spans of _____ days.

ⓐ .001 ⓑ .5 ⓒ 2 ⓓ 7

 Name four of the five most populated states.

 Which president of the United States said the following quote?

"The only thing we have to fear is fear itself."

 If a kangaroo can hop at a speed of *n* miles per hour, what is its speed in feet per hour?

 A cockroach can live _____ without a head.

ⓐ several minutes ⓑ several hours
ⓒ up to a day ⓓ weeks

Score: ___ / 7

Challenge 49

What is the measure of angle b?

Ⓐ 90°   Ⓑ Impossible to tell
Ⓒ 180° minus angle a   Ⓓ 89°

What was the minimum wage in 1970?

Ⓐ $.75 per hour   Ⓑ $1.60 per hour
Ⓒ $2.25 per hour   Ⓓ $2.70 per hour

There are 206 bones in the human body.
What percent of the 206 bones are hand and foot bones?

Ⓐ 20%   Ⓑ 40%   Ⓒ 50%   Ⓓ 75%

Name three of the five least populated states.

Which president of the United States said the following two quotes?

"A statesman is a politician who's been dead 10 or 15 years."

"It's a recession when your neighbor loses his job;
it's a depression when you lose yours."

If a kangaroo can hop at a speed of n miles per hour,
what is its speed in feet per minute?

What is the approximate weight of a paper clip?

Ⓐ 1 milligram   Ⓑ 10 milligrams
Ⓒ 1 gram   Ⓓ 10 grams

Score: ___ / 7

Challenge 50

What is the speed of a car if it travels one mile in 40 seconds?

If you work a 40-hour week for 52 weeks at the current minimum wage of $7.25, what do you earn in a year?

Ⓐ $10,000   Ⓑ $15,000   Ⓒ $20,000   Ⓓ $25,000

What is another name for the breastbone?

Canada has ten provinces and three territories. Name six.

Which president of the United States said the following quote?

"We look forward to a world founded upon four essential human freedoms. The first is freedom of speech and expression everywhere in the world. The second is freedom of every person to worship God in his own way-everywhere in the world. The third is freedom from want. ... The fourth is freedom from fear."

If a kangaroo can hop at a speed of n miles per hour, what is its speed in feet per second?

The record for the longest scientifically documented period without sleep is:

Ⓐ 78 hours   Ⓑ 96 hours
Ⓒ 114 hours   Ⓓ 264 hours

Score: ___ / 7

Challenge 51

A circular sprinkler at the center of a square garden waters every part of the garden except the corners. If the garden is a square with sides of 20 feet, how many square feet of the garden does the sprinkler not water?

The median U.S. wage in 2010 was $26,363. If it is assumed that this is for a 40-hour week, what is the hourly wage when one is paid $26,363 per year?

Ⓐ $10.50   Ⓑ $12.65   Ⓒ $14.20   Ⓓ $15.85

Tell whether each of the following is a base or an acid:

Ⓐ Bleach   Ⓑ Vinegar   Ⓒ Peanut Butter   Ⓓ Drain Cleaner

If the earth's population continues to double every 40 years, how many years will it be until the weight of all people on the earth is equal to the weight/mass of the entire earth?

Ⓐ 1500 years   Ⓑ 15,000 years

Ⓒ 150,000 years   Ⓓ 150,000,000 years

The total number of voting members in the House of Representatives is set by law at_____.

Ⓐ 100   Ⓑ 435   Ⓒ 535   Ⓓ 635

If Lori travels at 55 mph for *n* hours, how far did she travel?
(Distance equals Speed x Time)

On a warm day, oxygen molecules travel at an average speed of:

Ⓐ 10 mph   Ⓑ 50 mph   Ⓒ 100 mph   Ⓓ 1000 mph

Score: ___ / 7

Challenge 52

In the sequence 1, 4, 9, 16, 25, the 6th number is 36. What is the 100th number?

Ⓐ 2000 Ⓑ Impossible to tell
Ⓒ 10,000 Ⓓ None of the above

A day after a snow storm, 1/2 the snow melted. The next day, 1/4 of the remaining snow melted. What fraction of the snow from the storm is now left?

Air is made up of many elements and compounds. The top three are nitrogen, oxygen and _____.

Ⓐ Argon Ⓑ Carbon dioxide Ⓒ Neon Ⓓ Helium

How long is the "Chunnel" between England and France?

Ⓐ 16.4 miles Ⓑ 22.4 miles Ⓒ 27.4 miles Ⓓ 31.4 miles

Each representative in the House of Representatives serves for a _____ term.

Ⓐ two-year Ⓑ four-year Ⓒ six-year Ⓓ eight-year

Sara travels at 55 mph for *n* hours. Daniel travels five more hours than Sara, but at a speed of 30 mph. How far did they each travel?

Category 5 hurricanes have wind speeds over:

Ⓐ 100 mph Ⓑ 125 mph Ⓒ 155 mph Ⓓ 275 mph

Score: ___ / 7

Now You Know 63

Challenge 53

How many miles does light travel in a year?

The weight of a million one dollar bills is equivalent to the weight of how many medium sized cars?

Ⓐ Over 100   Ⓑ Approximately 10
Ⓒ Approximately 5   Ⓓ Less than one

How many skin cells do humans lose each minute?

Ⓐ 400   Ⓑ 40,000   Ⓒ 400,000   Ⓓ 4,000,000

What percent of the world's population died during the flu pandemic of 1918?

Ⓐ 2-3%   Ⓑ 6-7%   Ⓒ 12-14%   Ⓓ 25-30%

Each U.S. state is represented by two senators, regardless of population. Senators serve _____ terms.

Ⓐ two-year   Ⓑ four-year   Ⓒ six-year   Ⓓ eight-year

Sara travels at 55 mph for n hours. Daniel travels five more hours than Sara, but at a speed of 30 mph.
How many hours until Daniel catches up with Sara?

F5 tornadoes have winds over:

Ⓐ 200 mph   Ⓑ 260 mph   Ⓒ 300 mph   Ⓓ 550 mph

Score: ___ / 7

Challenge 54

A light year is the distance light travels in a year. How far is a "sound year" in miles?
(Sound travels .2 miles per second.)

For the next 64 days, pennies are placed on the squares of a chess board. 1st square - 1 penny • 2nd square - 2 pennies 3rd square - 4 pennies • 4th square - 8 pennies • 5th square - 16 pennies The number of pennies will double each day. What is the height of the stack of pennies placed on the 64th square? (A penny is 1/16 inch thick.)

Ⓐ 4 inches   Ⓑ Approximately the height of the Empire State Building

Ⓒ It will almost reach the moon

Ⓓ It will be almost halfway to the star Alpha Centauri A

What is the largest living thing on earth?

Ⓐ A redwood tree in California   Ⓑ A fungus in Oregon

Ⓒ Blue whale   Ⓓ A eucalyptus tree in Australia

World War I claimed an estimated 16 million lives. How many lives were lost during the flu pandemic of 1918?

Ⓐ 50,000   Ⓑ 50,000,000   Ⓒ 500,000,000   Ⓓ 1,000,000,000

The United State's Senate has several exclusive powers. Which of the following powers does the United State's Senate not have?

Ⓐ Power to impeach the president
Ⓑ Must consent to treaties before they are ratified
Ⓒ Confirms cabinet members
Ⓓ Confirms U.S. Supreme Court nominees

If Distance = Speed x Time, what does Time equal?

What is the weight of a British stone in pounds?

Score: ___ / 7

Challenge 55

How many cups are in a gallon?
Ⓐ 16   Ⓑ 32   Ⓒ 8   Ⓓ 24

If $100 loses 10% of its value each year, how many years until the original $100 is worth less than $50?

The weight of a blue whale's heart is approximately 3000 times the weight of a human's heart. The weight of a blue whale's brain is _____ times the weight of a human's brain.
Ⓐ 5 times   Ⓑ 50 times   Ⓒ 500 times   Ⓓ 5000 times

Greenland is considered the world's largest island. What is the second largest island?

The Constitution requires that the president be at least _____ years old.
Ⓐ 30   Ⓑ 35
Ⓒ 40   Ⓓ No age requirement

Rachel starts a bike trip at the beginning of a bike trail and travels at 10 mph. Jon starts his bike trip two hours later at the same spot and travels at 15 mph. How long until Jon catches up with Rachel?
(Remember that Distance = Speed x Time)

How many breaths does a typical person take in a lifetime?
Ⓐ 600,000   Ⓑ 6,000,000
Ⓒ 600,000,000   Ⓓ 600,000,000,000

Score: ___ / 7

Challenge 56

 If sound and light had a race across a football field of 100 yards starting from one goal line to the other, how far would sound have traveled when light travels the 100 yards to win the race?

- Ⓐ 4 feet
- Ⓑ 4 inches
- Ⓒ .004 inches
- Ⓓ .0000004 inches

 If the exchange rate is one dollar equals .80 euros, how many dollars would you receive for one euro?

 The ratio of brain weight to body weight in a human is 1/40. What is the ratio of brain weight to body weight in a lion?

- Ⓐ 1/40
- Ⓑ 1/80
- Ⓒ 1/250
- Ⓓ 1/550

 What percent of Europe's population died from the Black Plague in the outbreak that occurred in the 1300's?

- Ⓐ 3% - 6%
- Ⓑ 12% - 18%
- Ⓒ 30% - 60%
- Ⓓ over 80%

 The amendments that most people are familiar with are the first and second amendments. What are they?

 If $E = mc^2$, then what does m equal?

 The gas mileage for a Toyota Prius is 51 miles per gallon. What is the mileage for an M1 Abrams Main Battle Tank?

- Ⓐ .6 mpg
- Ⓑ 1 mpg
- Ⓒ 1.6 mpg
- Ⓓ 2.6 mpg

Score: ___ / 7

Challenge 57

The probability of at least two people having matching birthdays in a group of 23 people is:

Ⓐ 1 in 2 Ⓑ 1 in 3 Ⓒ 1 in 4 Ⓓ 1 in 15

When mortgage interest rates were 3%, a bank told a family that it could afford a home up to a cost of $300,000. If mortgage interest rates climb to 9%, what price home can the same family afford? (30 year mortgage)

Ⓐ $100,000 Ⓑ $150,000 Ⓒ $200,000 Ⓓ $250,000

While awake, a human brain generates enough power to light a:

Ⓐ 15-watt light bulb Ⓑ 60-watt light bulb
Ⓒ 75-watt light bulb Ⓓ 100-watt light bulb

The Mt. St. Helens eruption changed the lives of thousands of people and turned millions of acres of forest into a wasteland. When did Mt. St. Helens erupt?

Ⓐ 1960 Ⓑ 1970 Ⓒ 1980 Ⓓ 1990

Before the Pony Express, it took mail a month to travel from Missouri to California by stagecoach. The Pony Express took ____ days to travel from Missouri to California.

Ⓐ 4 Ⓑ 10 Ⓒ 22 Ⓓ 36

Use the formula for changing Celsius into Fahrenheit to find a formula for changing Fahrenheit into Celsius.

Fahrenheit = Celsius x 1.8 + 32   Celsius = ?

The gas tank capacity of a Toyota Prius is 11.9 gallons. What is the gas tank capacity of an M1 Abrams Main Battle Tank?

Ⓐ 50 gallons Ⓑ 150 gallons Ⓒ 300 gallons Ⓓ 500 gallons

Score: ___ / 7

Challenge 58

Is n^2 ever smaller than n?

Ⓐ Never Ⓑ Only when n is a fraction between 0 and 1
Ⓒ Only in bases other than base 10
Ⓓ Only when n is negative

How much did the space shuttle program cost each of the 313,000,000 people in the United States? (divided evenly)

Ⓐ $75   Ⓑ $675   Ⓒ $2175   Ⓓ $5275

Humans have a ratio of brain weight to body weight of 1/40. Match the following animals with their ratio of brain weight to body weight:
Cat - Shark - Small bird
1/2500   1/12   1/100

Norilsk, Russia is the northern most city in the world. What is its average temperature?

Ⓐ -10°F   Ⓑ -1°F   Ⓒ 9°F   Ⓓ 18°F

What is the salary for members of the House of Representatives and the Senate?

Ⓐ $124,000   Ⓑ $154,000   Ⓒ $174,000   Ⓓ $224,000

The number of cats is n; the number of dogs is $2n$ and the number of ostriches is $4n$. How many total legs are there?

Humans use _____ of their brains.

Ⓐ 10%   Ⓑ 25%   Ⓒ 50%   Ⓓ 100%

Score: ___ / 7

Challenge 59

What is the probability of rolling 5 of a kind when 5 dice are rolled?

Ⓐ 1/36 Ⓑ 1/216 Ⓒ 1/1296 Ⓓ 1/7776

A family in the United States spends, on average, what percent of its income on food each year?
(Food at home and away)

Ⓐ 13% Ⓑ 20% Ⓒ 27% Ⓓ 34%

Female tarantulas live 30 years or longer.
How long do male tarantulas live?

Ⓐ 40-50 years Ⓑ Same as females
Ⓒ 5-10 years Ⓓ Under a year

If all the Arctic ice melts, how high will the sea level rise?

Ⓐ It won't rise Ⓑ 12 feet Ⓒ 21 feet Ⓓ 35 feet

The House of Representatives has several exclusive powers.
Which of the following powers does the House of Representatives not have?

Ⓐ Power to initiate revenue bills
Ⓑ Power to impeach the president
Ⓒ Power to put the president on trial
Ⓓ Power to elect the president in case of an Electoral College deadlock

A cube has sides that are *n* inches long.
What is the volume of the cube?

The normal temperature for the human body is 98.6°F.
The highest human body temperature ever recorded was:

Ⓐ 106.8° F Ⓑ 108.6° F Ⓒ 110.6° F Ⓓ 115.7° F

Score: ___ / 7

Challenge 60

If a die is rolled three separate times, what is the probability that you will not roll any "4"s?

Ⓐ 91/216 Ⓑ 1/6 Ⓒ 1/2 Ⓓ 125/216

Before the Civil War, the average Southern family spent 6-7 dollars a month on food. By 1864, this increased to _____ per month.

Ⓐ $50-$60 Ⓑ $90-$100 Ⓒ $300 Ⓓ $400

Name Newton's first law of motion.

Where is the driest place on earth?

Ⓐ Top of Mount Everest Ⓑ Sahara Desert
Ⓒ Mohave Desert Ⓓ Antarctica

Which amendment allows a citizen to refuse to testify against him or herself?

A person with $1,000,000 gives $100 to a charity. How much should a person with *n* dollars donate to charity to give the same proportional amount?

How far apart are railroad tracks?

Ⓐ 4 feet 8.5 inches Ⓑ 5 feet 5.5 inches
Ⓒ 6 feet 6.5 inches Ⓓ 8 feet 2.5 inches

Score: ___ / 7

Challenge 61

How many cubic inches are in a cubic yard?

What is 1/4% of $100?

A human has a heart that is approximately 1% the size of a human body. The size of a blue whale heart is what percent of the entire whale?

Ⓐ 1%   Ⓑ 3%   Ⓒ 5%   Ⓓ 10%

When did Hawaii become a state?

Ⓐ 1919   Ⓑ 1939   Ⓒ 1959   Ⓓ 1969

Each state receives representation in the House of Representatives in proportion to its population, but is entitled to at least one representative. The most populous state, California, currently has 53 representatives. How many states only have one representative in the House of Representatives?

Ⓐ 1   Ⓑ 3   Ⓒ 5   Ⓓ 7

Juan's expenses for a dinner are $12 for a taxi, n dollars for a meal plus a 15% tip for the waitress. What is the total cost of the dinner plus taxi?

Red blood cells were discovered by Jan Swammerdam in ___.

Ⓐ 1658   Ⓑ 1728
Ⓒ 1758   Ⓓ 1828

Score: ___ / 7

Challenge 62

What is 1/2 of 1/2 of 1/2 of 1/2?

An ad for a "gold" coin says that for $19.95 you can get a genuine gold clad coin that contains a full 14 milligrams of gold. If gold cost $1500 per ounce, what is the value of 14 milligrams of gold?

Ⓐ 75 cents   Ⓑ $2.50   Ⓒ $15.00   Ⓓ $180.00

The heaviest documented primate on record belongs to what species?

Alaska was purchased for _____ dollars in 1867.

Ⓐ 100,000   Ⓑ 1.2 million
Ⓒ 7.2 million   Ⓓ 104 million

Each state receives representation in the House of Representatives in proportion to its population, but is entitled to at least one representative. The most populous state, California, currently has 53 representatives. There are currently seven states with only one representative. Name five.

There are a total of 19 grasshoppers and tarantulas. If the number of grasshoppers is called n, how many tarantula eyes are there? How many tarantula legs?

The mammal with the fastest heartbeat is the pygmy shrew. The mammal with the slowest heartbeat is the blue whale. What is the ratio of the heartbeat of a pygmy shrew to the heartbeat of a blue whale?

pygmy / blue whale =

Ⓐ 10/1   Ⓑ 50/1   Ⓒ 150/1   Ⓓ 2000/1

Score: ___ / 7

Challenge 63

A cubic decimeter of water weighs one kilogram.
What is the weight of a cubic meter of water?

Put in order from smallest to largest:

$.06   .07 cents   8 cents

The earth rotates at a speed of 1000 miles per hour.
How fast does the moon rotate?

Ⓐ 10 mph   Ⓑ 100 mph   Ⓒ 1000 mph   Ⓓ 10,000 mph

Alaska was purchased from Russia in 1867. What was the price per acre?

Ⓐ .5 cents   Ⓑ 2 cents   Ⓒ 14 cents   Ⓓ 37 cents

The amendments listed below are all included in the Bill of Rights.
Name the number for each amendment.

1) Right to a speedy trial, witnesses, etc.
2) Right to a trial by jury
3) Outlaws excessive bail and cruel punishment

The price of a book after a 15% discount is $8.5n$.
What was the original price of the book?

How many new cells does the human body make each day?

Ⓐ 24 million   Ⓑ 240,000,000

Ⓒ 2.4 billion   Ⓓ 24 billion

Score: ___ / 7

Challenge 64

You are facing a cliff that is an unknown distance away. If you shout towards the cliff, it takes 15 seconds for the echo to reach your ears. How far away is the cliff?

- Ⓐ 1.5 miles
- Ⓑ 3 miles
- Ⓒ 7.5 miles
- Ⓓ 15 miles

If apples are .60 cents each, what is the cost of 5 apples?

- Ⓐ 3 cents
- Ⓑ 3 dollars
- Ⓒ .30 dollars
- Ⓓ 30 cents

How many cells are in a typical human body?

- Ⓐ 100 billion
- Ⓑ One trillion
- Ⓒ 5 - 10 trillion
- Ⓓ 50 - 100 trillion

Name the state where each mountain is located.

Mt. McKinley   Pikes Peak   Mt. Ranier

Put the following inventions in order from earliest invented to most recent:

- Ⓐ Telephone
- Ⓑ Matches
- Ⓒ Lighter
- Ⓓ Hot air balloon

A painting and a frame together cost $800. If the painting cost $700 more than the frame, what is the cost of the frame?

Gold is so malleable that a small amount can be stretched very far. How long a wire can be made from one ounce of gold?

- Ⓐ 400 yards
- Ⓑ 1.5 miles
- Ⓒ 3.5 miles
- Ⓓ 62 miles

Score: __ / 7

Challenge 65

A microsecond is a millionth of a second and a picosecond is a trillionth of a second. What part of a microsecond is a picosecond?

Two cars each travel 15,000 miles each year. One gets 50 miles per gallon of gas while the other gets 40 miles per gallon. If gas cost $4.00 per gallon, how much less money does gas cost in the 50 mpg car? (for one year)

How many watts are in a kilowatt?

Name the state where each mountain is located.

Mt. Hood   Mt. Washington   Mt. St. Helens

An estimated _____ Americans died during the flu pandemic of 1918-1919.

Ⓐ 25,000   Ⓑ 75,000   Ⓒ 675,000   Ⓓ 5.25 million

A hill was climbed at a speed of n miles per hour. The descent was at a speed of $3n$ mph. What was the average speed for the entire trip?

The earth gets heavier every day because of falling space dust. How much heavier does the earth get each day?

Ⓐ 1 ton   Ⓑ 100 tons

Ⓒ 1,000,000 tons   Ⓓ 10 trillion tons

Score: ___ / 7

Challenge 66

If 28 people each ate 3/4 of a pie,
how many pies did they eat?

An apple and a pear together cost 90 cents.
If the apple cost twice as much as the pear, what did the apple cost?

What is the life span of a red blood cell?

  Ⓐ 14 days   Ⓑ 120 days   Ⓒ 18 months   Ⓓ 100 years

Some states have capitals that are not their largest city,
and because of this, many people answer incorrectly when asked
for those states' capitals. What are the capitals of the following states:
(Answer three out of the four correctly)

  Alaska   California   Illinois   Michigan

Polio epidemics increased in size and frequency in the late 1940's and
early 1950's before the introduction of the polio vaccine. On average,
how many cases of polio occurred each year in the
United States in the 1940's and early 50's before the polio vaccine?

  Ⓐ 3500   Ⓑ 35,000   Ⓒ 350,000   Ⓓ 3,500,000

There are five consecutive even numbers.
If the first is n, what are the other four?

17,228 players have played baseball in the major leagues.
What percent made it to the Hall of Fame?

  Ⓐ .35%   Ⓑ 1.35%   Ⓒ 3.35%   Ⓓ 7.35%

Score: ___ / 7

Challenge 67

What is 1/10 divided by 1/100?

A store is having a sale with discounts as shown below.
If the regular price starts at $100 on Sunday,
what will the price be on Friday?
Sunday: Regular price
Monday: 80% off
Tuesday: Additional 75% off Monday's price
Wednesday: Additional 20% off Tuesday's price
Thursday: Additional 50% off Wednesday's price
Friday: Additional 50% off Thursday's price

What is the life span of a white blood cell?
  Ⓐ 14 days   Ⓑ 120 days   Ⓒ 18 months   Ⓓ 100 years

Some states have capitals that are not their largest city, and because of this, many people answer incorrectly when asked for those states' capitals. What are the capitals of the following states:
(Answer three out of the four correctly)

  Nevada   Pennsylvania   Texas   Washington

All of the following have had polio except one. Name him or her.

Francis Ford Coppola	Donald Sutherland	Franklin Roosevelt
Joni Mitchell	Dustin Hoffman	Jack Nicklaus
Neil Young	Judy Collins	Itzhak Perlman

$x=y^2$
There are five consecutive odd numbers.
If the first is n, what are the other four?

The average barometric pressure at sea level is 29.92 inches of mercury.
What is the lowest barometric pressure ever recorded on earth?
  Ⓐ 11.74 inches of mercury   Ⓑ 25.69 inches of mercury
  Ⓒ 30.08 inches of mercury   Ⓓ 37.92 inches of mercury

Score: ___ / 7

Challenge 68

One definition of a meter is:
"The distance light travels in 1/299,792,458 of a second."
How many meters will light travel in one second?

What fraction of Americans own their home?

    Ⓐ 2/3   Ⓑ 1/3   Ⓒ 1/2   Ⓓ 1/4

What is the life span of a liver cell?

  Ⓐ 14 days   Ⓑ 120 days   Ⓒ 18 months   Ⓓ 100 years

How many square miles was the largest iceberg on record?
(Square miles above the water level)

    Ⓐ 60 square miles   Ⓑ 602 square miles

    Ⓒ 1602 square miles   Ⓓ 4,200 square miles.

During the period known as The Dark Ages, Rome and other cities deteriorated because of the invasions of barbarians from northern and central Europe. The term Dark Ages refers to the five hundred years following the fall of Rome. What time period was it?

    Ⓐ 150 AD - 650 AD   Ⓑ 500 AD - 1000 AD

    Ⓒ 850 AD - 1350 AD   Ⓓ 1250 AD - 1750 AD

On September 15, 2010, Luke is twice as old as Rachel who is twice as old as Daniel. If Daniel is n, then what will Luke's age be on September 15, 2013?

The average barometric pressure at sea level is 29.92 inches of mercury. What is the highest barometric pressure ever recorded on earth?

  Ⓐ 32.01   Ⓑ 33.42   Ⓒ 36.71   Ⓓ 39.21

Score: ___ / 7

Challenge 69

If the radius of a circle is cut in half, the area of the new circle is what fraction of the original circle?

A credit card is used to charge a $500 computer. If the annual interest rate is 34.9% and only the minimum monthly payment of $15 is paid, how long will it take to pay off the credit card debt?

Ⓐ 2 years   Ⓑ 5 years   Ⓒ 10 years   Ⓓ 121 years

What is the life span of a nerve cell?

Ⓐ 14 days   Ⓑ 120 days   Ⓒ 18 months   Ⓓ 100 years

What is the combined population of Canada and Mexico?

Ⓐ 147 million   Ⓑ 247 million
Ⓒ 347 million   Ⓓ 447 million

In what year did the Battle of the Alamo take place?

Ⓐ 1818   Ⓑ 1836   Ⓒ 1856   Ⓓ 1876

A blue whale is 5 times the weight of a brontosaurus, which is 7 times the weight of a tyrannosaurus rex. If the combined weight of all three is 215 tons, what does the tyrannosaurus rex weigh?

As the altitude increases, the oxygen content of the air decreases dramatically. At the top of Mount Everest, there is what fraction of the oxygen in the air as compared to sea level?

Ⓐ 3/4   Ⓑ 1/2   Ⓒ 1/3   Ⓓ 1/4

Score: ___ / 7

Challenge 70

If a ruler has a shadow of 4 inches,
how long a shadow would a yardstick have?

A credit card is used to charge a $500 computer. If the annual interest rate is 29.9% and only the minimum monthly payment of $13.14 is paid, the debt will be paid off in 10 years. How much total interest will be paid for the $500 loan?

Ⓐ $277.28   Ⓑ $577.28   Ⓒ $1077.28   Ⓓ $10,077.28

Trees receive an estimated _____ percent of their nutrition from the atmosphere and ____ percent from the soil.

Ⓐ 90% -- 10%   Ⓑ 10% -- 90%

Ⓒ 60% -- 40%   Ⓓ 30% -- 70%

The United States has 50 states while Canada has 10 provinces and 3 territories. How is Mexico divided?

Ⓐ It has three large states   Ⓑ It has 31 states

Ⓒ It is not divided into provinces or states   Ⓓ It is divided into 7 regions

What year did the Battle of the Little Bighorn (Custer's Last Stand) take place?

Ⓐ 1796   Ⓑ 1816   Ⓒ 1876   Ⓓ 1896

Car rental company A charges $40 per day plus 8 cents per mile. Car rental company B charges $120 per day, but does not charge for miles driven. How many miles must one drive to have the charges from both companies be the same?

The record height for a parachute jump is:

Ⓐ 3.6 miles   Ⓑ 6.8 miles   Ⓒ 11.4 miles   Ⓓ 19.5 miles

Score: ___ / 7

Challenge 71

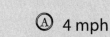

If you walked up a hill at a speed of 3 miles per hour and then down the same path at a speed of 6 miles per hour, what would be your average speed for your walk?

Ⓐ 4 mph Ⓑ 4.5 mph

Ⓒ It is impossible to tell without a distance Ⓓ 5 mph

A $25,000 car cost $27,250 when sales tax is added. What is the sales tax rate?

How much would a person who weighs 200 pounds on earth weigh on a neutron star?

Ⓐ Same Ⓑ 2800 pounds

Ⓒ 280,000 pounds Ⓓ 28,000,000,000,000 pounds

Put these places in order from north to south:
Northern tip of Maine -- London -- Halifax, Nova Scotia.

Ⓐ Northern tip of Maine; London; Halifax, Nova Scotia
Ⓑ London; Northern tip of Maine; Halifax, Nova Scotia
Ⓒ London; Halifax, Nova Scotia; Northern tip of Maine
Ⓓ Halifax, Nova Scotia; Northern tip of Maine; London

Terrible conditions for children who worked in factories in England in the 1830's led to laws that protected child workers. One 1830's law said that no one under the age of _____ could work in factories.

Ⓐ 7 years old Ⓑ 9 years old Ⓒ 12 years old Ⓓ 15 years old

If a 10' by 50' wall can be painted in 5 hours, how much of the wall can be painted in *n* hours?

What planet has the longest day and which one has the shortest day?

Score: ___ / 7

Challenge 72

50% of the students at Glenwood University are women;
25% of the women play chess;
10% of the women who play chess are experts;
50% of the women experts are left-handed.
If 10 of the women chess experts are left-handed,
how many students attend Glenwood University?

Ⓐ 160 Ⓑ 1600 Ⓒ 1000 Ⓓ None of the above

What is the cost of smoking two packs of cigarettes a day for a year if you live in New York City and buy your cigarettes there?

Ⓐ $2,350 Ⓑ $5,450 Ⓒ $6,850 Ⓓ $10,950

How much would a person who weighs 200 pounds on earth weigh on our sun?

Ⓐ 500 pounds Ⓑ 2500 pounds
Ⓒ 5500 pounds Ⓓ 10,000,000 pounds

The Richter Scale is a way to quantify the energy contained in an earthquake. The difference in ground motion between a magnitude 6 earthquake and a magnitude 8 earthquake is how many times stronger in a magnitude 8 earthquake?

A child labor law passed in the 1840's in England said that children under the age of 13 could work no more than _____ hours per week.

Ⓐ 12 Ⓑ 24 Ⓒ 36 Ⓓ 48

A television that normally sells for n dollars is on sale for 25% off. What is the total price for the television if the sales tax rate is 6%?

What is the height of the world's tallest building? (Dubai)

Ⓐ 1832 feet Ⓑ 2723 feet
Ⓒ 3361 feet Ⓓ 1 mile 132 feet

Score: ___ / 7

Challenge 73

 How many cubic yards of cement will be used in a driveway that is 3 yards wide, 9 yards long and one foot thick?

 The bill for groceries was $18.37. The clerk was given a $20 bill and 2 quarters. What is the change?

 The Amazon rain forest produces what percent of the world's oxygen?
    Ⓐ 20%   Ⓑ 40%   Ⓒ 60%   Ⓓ 80%

 The number of children per woman is highest in what country?
    Ⓐ India   Ⓑ South Africa   Ⓒ Niger   Ⓓ Saudi Arabia

 What year was the D-Day Invasion at Normandy?
    Ⓐ 1941   Ⓑ 1943   Ⓒ 1944   Ⓓ 1946

If Keith types 80 words per minute and there are 160 words on a page, how many minutes would it take Keith to type n pages?

 How many atoms are in the entire universe?
    Ⓐ 10^{87} Ⓑ 10^{5000} Ⓒ $10^{500,000}$ Ⓓ $10^{87,000,000,000,000,000,000}$

Score: __ / 7

Challenge 74

If a building is 20 feet tall and the base of a ladder is 15 feet from the building, how long is the ladder?

Ⓐ 25 feet Ⓑ 22.5 feet
Ⓒ Impossible to tell Ⓓ 22 feet

A person with $1,000,000 gives $100 to a charity. How much should a person with $1000 donate to charity to give the same proportional amount?

The unit of measure for weight in the United States is the pound. What unit is used for mass?

Ⓐ Newton Ⓑ Kilogram/gram Ⓒ Stone Ⓓ Slug

One of the longest bridges in the world is the Danyang-Kunshan Grand Bridge in China. How long is it?

Ⓐ 5.5 miles Ⓑ 8.5 miles Ⓒ 20 miles Ⓓ 102.4 miles

Four U.S. presidents have been assassinated while in office. Name three.

If Keith types 80 words per minute and there are 160 words on a page, how many hours would it take Keith to type *n* pages?

How long would it take for a penny dropped from the Empire State Building to hit the ground?

Ⓐ 2 seconds Ⓑ 5 seconds Ⓒ 9 seconds Ⓓ 23 seconds

Score: ___ / 7

Challenge 75

10^{10} is how many times larger than 10^9?

- (A) 10,000 times
- (B) 1000 times
- (C) 100 times
- (D) 10 times

If an American went to Germany and saw that lunch was 8 euros, how many dollars would the lunch cost?
Exchange rate: 1 Euro = 1.2771 U.S. dollars

The unit of measure for weight in the United States is the pound. What is the unit of weight in the metric system?

- (A) Newton
- (B) Kilogram/gram
- (C) Stone
- (D) Slug

What is the largest city in China?

- (A) Beijing
- (B) Hong Kong
- (C) Shanghai
- (D) Tianjin

Who were the leaders of the three Allied countries during World War II? (U.S., England and Russia)

The formula for finding the temperature (Celsius) based on the number of cricket chirps per minute is:

$$\text{Celsius} = \frac{\text{chirps per minute} + 30}{7}$$

What is the formula for predicting the number of cricket chirps if you know the temperature?   Chirps per minute = ?

How tall is the Empire State Building with its antenna spire included?

- (A) 1454 feet
- (B) 1986 feet
- (C) 2341 feet
- (D) 2834 feet

Score: ___ / 7

Challenge 76

It is almost impossible to fold a paper more than 7 or 8 times, but if it were possible, how thick would a 1/32 of an inch piece of paper be if you folded it 50 times?
(It will be 2/32 of an inch after it is folded once; 4/32 of an inch after it is folded twice; 8/32 after three folds; etc.)

Ⓐ 8 inches   Ⓑ 3 feet   Ⓒ 18.2 feet   Ⓓ More than 50 feet

If a German came to New York City and saw that a Broadway show cost $110, how many euros would she expect to pay?
Exchange rate: 1 Euro = 1.2771 U.S. dollars

Put the following animals in order from slowest heartbeat to fastest.

Elephant   Hibernating bear

Blue whale   Human

Where is the world's deepest lake?

Ⓐ Lake Baikal - Russia   Ⓑ Tanganika - Tanzania
Ⓒ Caspian Sea - Iran, Russia, others
Ⓓ Lake Superior - United States, Canada

In what year did Adolf Hitler come to power?

Ⓐ 1923   Ⓑ 1928   Ⓒ 1933   Ⓓ 1938

If a heart beats 72 times per minute, how many times does it beat in n seconds?

Subtract the average height of a female in the United States from the average height of a male in the United States: _____ inches

Ⓐ 3.4 inches   Ⓑ 4.4 inches   Ⓒ 5.4 inches   Ⓓ 6.4 inches

Score: ___ / 7

Challenge 77

Is 5n ever larger than 10n?
- Ⓐ Never
- Ⓑ Only when n is a fraction
- Ⓒ Only in bases other than base 10
- Ⓓ Yes

A Japanese visitor to Paris sees that hotel rooms cost 212 euros per night. How many yen would he need to pay? (round to the nearest yen)

Exchange rate: 1 Euro = 1.2771 U.S. dollars
1 U.S. dollar = 76.7833 yen

There are currently approximately _____ known animal species upon planet earth.
- Ⓐ 100,000
- Ⓑ 5 - 10 million
- Ⓒ 50 - 100 million
- Ⓓ 1 - 2 billion

How deep is the world's deepest lake?
- Ⓐ 1253 feet
- Ⓑ 2314 feet
- Ⓒ 5369 feet
- Ⓓ 6.34 miles

World War I went from 1914 to 1918. In what year did the United States enter the war?
- Ⓐ 1914
- Ⓑ 1915
- Ⓒ 1916
- Ⓓ 1917

If the value of a pile of coins is 82n cents, what is the value of the coins expressed as dollars?

The world's longest snake was a reticulated python, which was found in Indonesia in 1912. How long was it?
- Ⓐ 23.75 feet
- Ⓑ 32.75 feet
- Ⓒ 40.75 feet
- Ⓓ 49 feet

Score: ___ / 7

Challenge 78

$1/2 + 1/4 + 1/8 + 1/16 + 1/32 + ... =$

- Ⓐ Infinity
- Ⓑ Impossible to tell
- Ⓒ Approaches 1
- Ⓓ Is a number between 1 and 2

There are 500 marbles in a box. The value of a red marble is 10 cents and the value of a blue marble is 25 cents. When 50 marbles are drawn randomly from the box, there are 40 blue and 10 red marbles. Estimate the value of the box of marbles.

Meteors move very fast with some entering the earth's atmosphere at speeds as high as:

- Ⓐ The speed of sound
- Ⓑ 3000 miles per hour
- Ⓒ 130,000 miles per hour
- Ⓓ The speed of light

The deepest hole ever drilled by man is the Kola Superdeep Borehole (Russia). How deep was it?

- Ⓐ 2.6 miles
- Ⓑ 7.6 miles
- Ⓒ 29.6 miles
- Ⓓ 53.6 miles

India gained freedom from British rule in:

- Ⓐ 1907
- Ⓑ 1927
- Ⓒ 1947
- Ⓓ 1967

In a pile of nickels, dimes and quarters, there are 10 times as many quarters as dimes and twice as many dimes as nickels. If the value of the coins is $36.75, how many quarters are there?

A 1985 study conducted by the science journal 'Nature' calculated the rate of meteorites hitting humans as once every _____.

- Ⓐ 1.8 years
- Ⓑ 25 years
- Ⓒ 105 years
- Ⓓ 180 years

Score: ___ / 7

Challenge 79

A water pipe with an eight inch diameter is replaced with one with a four inch diameter. By how much is the flow reduced through the pipe?

    Ⓐ 1/2 the water   Ⓑ 3/4 the water

    Ⓒ 1/4 the water   Ⓓ 1/8 the water

How much more interest would be earned if $8000 is invested for a year at 9% interest instead of 3% interest?

There are 8 main blood types in humans. Name six of the eight.

Which country has the lowest life expectancy? (United Nations data)

    Ⓐ Mozambique   Ⓑ Afghanistan

    Ⓒ Zimbabwe   Ⓓ Somalia

Match the person with his country:

Napoleon	Gandhi	Karl Marx	Czar Romanov
Russia	*Germany*	*India*	*France*

How many toes are in a group of *n* people?

Humans have 46 chromosomes. A type of fern called adders-tongue (Ophioglossum reticulatum) has the highest known number of chromosomes. How many chromosomes does this plant have?

  Ⓐ 84   Ⓑ 242   Ⓒ 342   Ⓓ Over 1000

Score: ___ / 7

Challenge 80

If a die is rolled three separate times, what is the probability that at least one "4" will be rolled?
Ⓐ 91/216   Ⓑ 1/6   Ⓒ 1/2   Ⓓ 125/216

If $5000 is charged on a credit card that charges 34.9% interest, how much is the interest charge for one year?

Dry ice consists of solid _____.

Put these cities in order from west to east: San Francisco, Reno, Los Angeles.
Ⓐ San Francisco, Reno, Los Angeles
Ⓑ Reno, Los Angeles, San Francisco
Ⓒ San Francisco, Los Angeles, Reno
Ⓓ Los Angeles, San Francisco, Reno

When was the California gold rush?
Ⓐ 1749   Ⓑ 1801   Ⓒ 1849   Ⓓ 1901

A child is holding a box of coins that contains the same number of pennies, nickels, dimes, quarters, half dollars and silver dollars. If the value of the money in the box is $22.92, how many quarters are in the box?

The space shuttle travels about _____ times faster than a bullet.
Ⓐ About the same   Ⓑ 5 times faster
Ⓒ 20 times faster   Ⓓ 100 times faster

Score: ___ / 7

Challenge 81

When 36 gallons are poured into an empty tank, it will be 3/4 full. How many gallons does the tank hold?

Six presidents are portrayed on U.S. coins. Name five.
(Ignore presidential dollars that have been issued starting in 2007.)

Answer two of these facts about rocks and minerals.

Hardest natural substance found on earth is:_____
Most common rock in the earth's crust is:_____
What type of rock forms when magma cools and solidifies? _____

How many time zones are in the continental United States?

What is the name of the Prime Minister of India who was assassinated on October 31, 1984?

Eric is half his father's height. Eric's pet dog is half Eric's height and also twice the height of Eric's pet cat.
Eric's hamster is 1/4 the height of the cat.
If Eric's and the hamster's height total 34 inches, how tall is Eric?

Baseball teams often "retire" numbers when a star player ends his career. For example, 9 teams have retired the number "5". This means that no other player will ever wear that number for that team.
Of the first 50 numbers, how many numbers have been "retired" by at least one team?

Ⓐ 24 out of 50   Ⓑ 34 out of 50
Ⓒ 46 out of 50   Ⓓ 50 out of 50

Score: ___ / 7

Challenge 82

The largest gold nugget was found at Moliagul, Victoria, Australia in 1869 and weighed approximately 156 pounds.
What size cube is closest to the volume of 156 pounds of gold?

Ⓐ 6 inch cube   Ⓑ Cubic foot   Ⓒ Cubic meter   Ⓓ Cubic decimeter

Name the person portrayed on each denomination of U.S. paper currency:

$1: $2: $5:

$10: $20: $50: $100:

Dry ice is extremely cold. Its temperature is:

Ⓐ -50°F   Ⓑ -109°F   Ⓒ -276°F   Ⓓ -459°F

Niagara Falls drains one of the Great Lakes into another Great Lake.
Name the two Great Lakes.

When did the first spacecraft land on Mars?

Ⓐ 1959   Ⓑ 1967   Ⓒ 1971   Ⓓ 1980

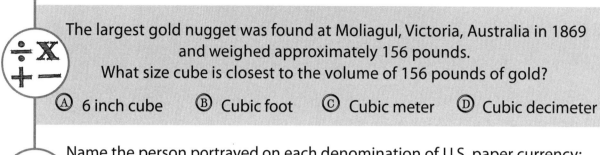
If there are n shoes in a closet,
how many pairs of shoes are in the closet?

How far above the earth did the space shuttle orbit?

Ⓐ 200-385 miles   Ⓑ 1200 - 2000 miles
Ⓒ 22,000 miles   Ⓓ Anywhere from 500 to 25,000 miles

Score: ___ / 7

Now You Know 93

Challenge 83

Put the following numbers in order from smallest to largest.
.10001
.0899462
.0997

Stan bought a car for n dollars and paid $1750 in sales tax.
Mark lives in a different state where the sales tax is 1% lower.
He paid the same amount for the car as Stan (n dollars) and then paid sales tax of $1500. What was the price of the car before sales tax?

Granite is a type of:

Ⓐ Igneous Rock   Ⓑ Sedimentary Rock

Ⓒ Metamorphic Rock   Ⓓ Jade

Name four of the five most populous countries in Europe.
(Include Russia in Europe)

How many years was the Unites States involved in the Vietnam War?

Ⓐ 5   Ⓑ 10   Ⓒ 15   Ⓓ 20

Flash ran n yards in 3 seconds.
How many inches did he run?

Geostationary satellites move in sync with the earth's orbit.
How high do they orbit?

Ⓐ 180 miles   Ⓑ 1840 miles

Ⓒ 22,400 miles   Ⓓ 52,400 miles

Score: ___ / 7

Challenge 84

How many different arrangements are possible with five pictures and five hooks?

A television that normally sells for $400 is on sale for 20% off. What is the total price for the television if the sales tax rate is 5%?

One of the animals below has roughly the same ratio of brain weight to body weight as a human.

Ⓐ Cat   Ⓑ Mouse   Ⓒ Shark   Ⓓ Small bird

How large is the largest land animal in the Antarctic?

Ⓐ 8 inches long   Ⓑ 4 inches long
Ⓒ 2 inches long   Ⓓ 1/2 inch long

Name four of the five United State's presidents who were in office during the Vietnam War.

If Flash runs at a pace of n feet per second, how many miles will he run in an hour?

The space shuttle's large external tank is loaded with more than _____ gallons of super-cold liquid oxygen and liquid hydrogen.

Ⓐ 5,000   Ⓑ 50,000   Ⓒ 500,000   Ⓓ 5,000,000

Score: ___ / 7

Challenge 85

A cube has a volume of 64 cubic feet. What is the length of each of its sides?

What is the percent of increase if a salary is increased from $60,000 to $75,000?

What percent of the motor cortex in the human brain (the part of the brain which controls all movement in the body) is devoted to the muscles of the hands?

Ⓐ 5%   Ⓑ 10%   Ⓒ 12%   Ⓓ 25%

What is the approximate population of Australia?

Ⓐ 23,000,000   Ⓑ 75,000,000
Ⓒ 125,000,000   Ⓓ 185,000,000

How long after General Lee surrendered was Lincoln assassinated?

Ⓐ 5 days   Ⓑ 4 months
Ⓒ One year, one month   Ⓓ Same day

What is the sum of three consecutive multiples of 5 if the smallest number is n?

How fast did the space shuttle travel?

Ⓐ 3000 mph   Ⓑ 12,500 mph
Ⓒ 17,500 mph   Ⓓ 25,500 mph

Score: ___ / 7

Challenge 86

Three pieces of pie are eaten as shown.
What fraction of the pie is left?
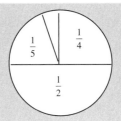

What is the percent of decrease if a salary is decreased from $75,000 to $60,000?

The colors of visible light are:
Red, Yellow, Blue, Violet, Orange, Green, Indigo
Which one has the longest wavelength
and which one has the shortest?

Luke is living in Kuwait. His mom, who lives in Chicago, wants to call him. Luke gets up at 5:00 A.M. and goes to bed at 7:00 P.M. Kuwait time. What would be a good time for Luke's mom to call him (Chicago time)?

Ⓐ 11:00 A.M.   Ⓑ 3:00 P.M.   Ⓒ 7:00 P.M.   Ⓓ 10:00 P.M.

How long after the Confederate defeat at Gettysburg did the Civil War end?

Ⓐ Approximately 2 months   Ⓑ Approximately 8 months
Ⓒ Approximately one year   Ⓓ Approximately two years

Alicia's salary is $5000 more than 1/4 of Dan's salary.
If Dan's salary is n, what is Alicia's salary?

How old was the youngest soldier to serve in the Civil War?

Ⓐ 8 years old   Ⓑ 9 years old
Ⓒ 11 years old   Ⓓ 13 years old

Score: ___ / 7

Challenge 87

Laura will roll one die two times. If she rolls a three with any roll, she wins $1,000,000. What is her probability of winning the $1,000,000?

Ⓐ 11/36 Ⓑ 1/3 Ⓒ 1/6 Ⓓ 1/36

A car uses one gallon of gas to travel 35 miles.
If gas cost $4 per gallon, what will it cost to take a 700 mile trip?

The use of chlorofluorocarbons (CFC's) has been phased out because of their ability to destroy the ozone layer. The destructive power of CFC's is illustrated by the fact that one chlorine atom can destroy up to _____ molecules of ozone.

Ⓐ 10,000 Ⓑ 100,000 Ⓒ 1,000,000 Ⓓ 100,000,000,000

What percent of the corn grown in the United States goes to the production of ethanol? (2011)

Ⓐ 10% Ⓑ 20% Ⓒ 30% Ⓓ 40%

How many voyages to the New World did Columbus make?

If a flea can jump n centimeters high, how many meters can it jump?

Put the following in order from shortest to tallest:
- Tallest redwood in California
- Great Pyramid near Cairo
- Statue of Liberty *(from ground to torch)*
- Washington Monument

Score: ___ / 7

Challenge 88

The length of a marathon is 26.2 miles.
If a runner traveled at a pace of 6 mph,
how many minutes would it take him/her to finish a marathon?

If 3 ounces of dark chocolate cost $1.50,
what does a pound of dark chocolate cost?

The boiling point of water is 212°F and the freezing point of water is 32°F.
What is the boiling and freezing point of water in the Celsius scale?

The wettest place in the United States is Mt. Waialeale in Hawaii.
It averages _____ inches of rain each year.

Ⓐ 100　　　Ⓑ 400　　　Ⓒ 900　　　Ⓓ 1300

Magellan started his journey around the world in 1519 with
five ships and 265 sailors. By the time the trip was done in 1522,
how many ships and sailors returned home?

Ⓐ 4 ships and 194 sailors　　　Ⓑ 3 ships and 157 sailors
Ⓒ 2 ships and 98 sailors　　　Ⓓ 1 ship and 18 sailors

If a kangaroo can jump n meters,
how many millimeters can it jump?

One silkworm's cocoon, when unfolded,
can have a piece of silk _____ feet long.

Ⓐ 30 feet　　Ⓑ 300 feet　　Ⓒ 3000 feet　　Ⓓ 30,000 feet

Score: ___ / 7

Challenge 89

If a person who is 6 feet tall has a shadow of 4 feet, how tall is a tree that casts a shadow of 24 feet?

If milk cost $6.40 per gallon, what does a cup of milk cost?

The Kelvin scale starts with a "0" at absolute zero. What is the boiling and freezing point of water in the Kelvin scale?

- Ⓐ 373.15 K and 273.15 K
- Ⓑ 612.15 K and 342.15 K
- Ⓒ 1000 K and 500 K
- Ⓓ 100 K and 0 K

The definition of a desert is: "A location that gets less than _____ of rain per year."

- Ⓐ 1 inch
- Ⓑ 2 inches
- Ⓒ 5 inches
- Ⓓ 10 inches

According to the U.S. Department of Agriculture, ___ percent of all land in the United States is owned by the Federal government.

- Ⓐ 8%
- Ⓑ 18%
- Ⓒ 29%
- Ⓓ over 50%

If you know your weight in pounds, you can find your mass by dividing by 32: mass = weight/32
If you know your mass, how do you find your weight?
weight =

How long do fingernails grow in a year?

- Ⓐ 1/4 inch
- Ⓑ 3/4 inch
- Ⓒ 1.5 inches
- Ⓓ 3.5 inches

Score: ___ / 7

Challenge 90

A meter is a little longer than a yard. A centimeter is equal to:

- Ⓐ About an inch
- Ⓑ Approximately 2.5 inches
- Ⓒ A little less than half an inch
- Ⓓ Close to 1/10 inch

What does it cost to keep a 100-watt bulb on for 24 hours when electricity cost 10 cents per kilowatt hour?

An average person at sea level has about 13-14 kilopascals (kPa) of oxygen in their bloodstream. University College of London medical researcher Dan Martin and three colleagues climbed Mount Everest and measured their own blood oxygen level near the summit. What happened to their oxygen level?

- Ⓐ Went up significantly
- Ⓑ About 20% lower than normal
- Ⓒ Lowest ever measured in live people
- Ⓓ About 30% lower than normal

The largest desert in the world is:

- Ⓐ Sahara
- Ⓑ Mojave
- Ⓒ Gobi
- Ⓓ Great Victoria

Who becomes president if both the president and vice-president die?

A car rental company charges $45 per day plus 11 cents per mile. If a car was rented for d days and driven m miles, what was the cost of the rental in dollars?

What percent of the world's population was on Facebook in 2012?

- Ⓐ 5%
- Ⓑ 15%
- Ⓒ 25%
- Ⓓ 30%

Score: ___ / 7

Challenge 91

 Convert the following base 5 decimal into a base 10 fraction: .4

- Ⓐ 4/10
- Ⓑ 4/5
- Ⓒ Can't be converted
- Ⓓ 1/4

 If $960 will last 12 days for 3 people. How long will it last if there are 4 people?

 The neural bridge that connects the two hemispheres to each other and is centrally located in the brain is called the:

- Ⓐ Hypothalamus
- Ⓑ Corpus Callosum
- Ⓒ Amygdala
- Ⓓ Hippocampus

 What is the average ocean temperature?

- Ⓐ 39°F
- Ⓑ 48°F
- Ⓒ 57°F
- Ⓓ 66°F

 How much tea was ruined during the Boston Tea Party?

- Ⓐ 100 pounds
- Ⓑ 1000 pounds
- Ⓒ 90,000 pounds
- Ⓓ No tea, but over 500 pounds of coffee

 Juan is paid $22.50 per hour and a bonus of $75 each week. If Juan was paid $862.50 one week, how many hours did he work?

What is the heaviest fruit?

Score: ___ / 7

Challenge 92

What is the probability of winning a 6 number lottery where the numbers range from 1-40?

Ⓐ 1/10,420   Ⓑ 1/100,682   Ⓒ 1/3,838,380

Ⓓ About the same as the probability of getting struck by lightning in a year

A friend offered to pay .50% of your $1500 dental bill. How much of the $1500 will be left after your friend's contribution?

Newborn human babies are typically 1/20 of the weight of the mother. What fraction of the mother's weight is a newborn kangaroo?

Ⓐ 1/20   Ⓑ 1/100   Ⓒ 1/1000   Ⓓ 1/50,000

What is the population of the world's least populated country?

Ⓐ 8   Ⓑ 800   Ⓒ 8000   Ⓓ 80,000

Who wrote the pamphlet "Common Sense"?

Ⓐ John Adams   Ⓑ Thomas Paine
Ⓒ Thomas Jefferson Ⓓ John Hancock

A barn contains cows, ducks, and a three-legged dog named Tripod. There are 5 times as many cows as ducks and a total of 333 legs. How many ducks are in the barn?

What were Aristotle's four elements?

Score: ___ / 7

Challenge 93

A science book incorrectly stated that the speed of light was approximately 300,000 miles per second. What is the most likely explanation for this mistake?

In 2010, Trevor's $100,000 salary was increased by 200%. In 2011, Trevor's salary was decreased by 100%. What is his salary now?

A blood pressure reading of 160/110 is:

Ⓐ Within the normal range   Ⓑ Borderline high
Ⓒ Low side of normal   Ⓓ Extremely high

How many Alaskas will fit into the lower 48 states?

Ⓐ 2   Ⓑ 3   Ⓒ 4   Ⓓ 5

Who wrote the first draft of The Declaration of Independence?

When each side of a square is tripled, the area increases by 392 square inches. What is the area of the original square?

Very large waves are called tsunamis. They can move at speeds as high as:

Ⓐ 30 miles per hour   Ⓑ 100 miles per hour
Ⓒ 500 miles per hour   Ⓓ 1000 miles per hour

Score: ___ / 7

Challenge 94

If the weight of a dozen donuts is 3 pounds, how many ounces does one donut weigh?

If you spend $15 per day for cigarettes, what will your total cost for cigarettes be if you smoke for 10 years? (365 days in a year)

On a summer afternoon, a car is traveling at a speed of 60 miles per hour. A ball is hanging inside the car as shown below. The driver slams on the brakes and skids to a stop to avoid a deer in the road. What happens to the hanging ball when the brakes are applied forcefully?

(roof of car is flat)

Ⓐ Moves slightly towards the back of the car
Ⓑ Does not move
Ⓒ Moves forward until it hits the top of the car
Ⓓ Moves forward, but will never hit the top of the car

How many miles is Hawaii from California?
Ⓐ 560 miles Ⓑ 1260 miles Ⓒ 1890 miles Ⓓ 2,390 miles

What was George Washington's annual salary while he was president?
Ⓐ $5000 Ⓑ $10,000 Ⓒ $15,000 Ⓓ $25,000

In the year 2000, Larry is twice as old as Curly.
Ten years later,
their ages add up to 53.
How old was Larry in the year 2000?

There are currently (2012) five official dwarf planets.
Name two.

Score: ___ / 7

Challenge 95

Stanley found a bag of money. He gave 1/2 to charity, 1/4 to his sister and 1/8 to his brother. Stanley now has $10 remaining. How much money was in the bag when he found it?

Four children inherited money from their parents. The oldest child received half the money while the second oldest received half of what was left. The youngest two then split the remaining money. If the youngest two each received $50,000, what was the total amount of money the four children inherited?

Which of the following is an optimal blood pressure?

Ⓐ 120/80 Ⓑ 140/80 Ⓒ 115/75

Ⓓ Any reading below 150/100

The Arctic and Antarctic circles are closest to which one of the following lines of latitude?

Ⓐ 57 Ⓑ 67 Ⓒ 75 Ⓓ 83

In what year was the Louisiana Purchase?

Ⓐ 1735 Ⓑ 1790 Ⓒ 1803 Ⓓ 1823

A store determined that in a year's time .1% of its checks were bad. If the store had 5 bad checks in a year's time, how many total checks did it receive during the year?

At the top of Pikes Peak, the oxygen in the air is _____ percent lower than at sea level.

Ⓐ 10% Ⓑ 25% Ⓒ 40% Ⓓ 50%

Score: ___ / 7

Challenge 96

A movie starts at 7:30 and goes until 10:00.
At what time is the movie 1/3 over?

A person with a net worth of $1000 gave $50 to charity.
How much should a person with a net worth of 10 billion dollars give to charity to give the same proportional amount?

The following sentence appeared in a science magazine:
"While liquid hydrogen is the densest form of the fuel, keeping it at the required 480 degrees below zero in the on-board storage tank is expensive and difficult."
What mistake did the author make?

The Tropics of Cancer and Capricorn lie parallel to the equator at about _____ latitude.

  Ⓐ 18°   Ⓑ 23°   Ⓒ 28°   Ⓓ 32°

The Louisiana Purchase increased the size of the United States by:

  Ⓐ 25%   Ⓑ 50%   Ⓒ 75%   Ⓓ 100%

If I add the page number of the book I am reading to the 3 previous pages, I get the number 374. What page am I reading?

The average temperature at 40,000 feet is approximately:

  Ⓐ -60° F   Ⓑ 0° F   Ⓒ 32° F   Ⓓ 95° F

Score: ___ / 7

Challenge 97

1/4 pound of gold is going to be shared by 4 people. How many ounces will each receive?

The charge to ride a taxi is a $5 flat fee plus $1.25 per mile plus a 20% tip. What would you pay for a 20 mile taxi ride?

The headline in a newspaper read:
"Flu vaccines are only 59% effective."
Which of the following sentences best explains the meaning of the headline?

Ⓐ If you get a flu vaccine, 59% of the time you will not get the flu.

Ⓑ If 100 people get the vaccine, approximately 59 will not get the flu and 41 will get the flu.

Ⓒ If you get the vaccine every year for the rest of your life, you will get the flu, on average, only 2 times for every 5 times an unvaccinated person gets the flu.

Ⓓ Without the flu vaccine, you are likely to get the flu.

In which continent is Buddhism a major religion?

Ⓐ Europe   Ⓑ Africa   Ⓒ South America   Ⓓ Asia

The United States paid France _____ per acre for all the land they acquired with the Louisiana Purchase.

Ⓐ .03 cents   Ⓑ 3 cents   Ⓒ 13 cents   Ⓓ 30 cents

If you multiply a certain number by 5, your answer is the same as when you add 144 to the number. What is the number?

As the altitude increases, the oxygen content of the air decreases dramatically. At 20,000 feet there is what fraction of the oxygen in the air when compared to sea level?

Ⓐ 3/4   Ⓑ 1/2   Ⓒ 1/3   Ⓓ 1/4

Score: ___ / 7

Challenge 98

A house that is 18 feet tall has a shadow of 3 feet.
If Dave has a shadow of 10 inches, how many feet tall is Dave?

A rent-to-own plan for a television requires a $75 monthly payment for two years. If the television was paid for with cash, it would cost $500. How much more money will a person pay using a rent-to-own plan compared to paying with cash?

The atmosphere is divided into four main sections. The troposphere is the lowest and has a typical temperature of 68° F. The next highest level is the stratosphere with a typical temperature of -60° F. The next is the mesosphere with a typical temperature of -90° F. The highest section of the atmosphere is the thermosphere. What is a typical temperature in the thermosphere?

Ⓐ -90° F   Ⓑ -120° F   Ⓒ -150° to -200° F   Ⓓ 1000° to 2000° F

There are five Great Lakes --- name four.

The following is at the very end of the _____ "that this nation under God shall have a new birth of freedom; and that government of the people, by the people, for the people, shall not perish from the earth."

Ⓐ Declaration of Independence   Ⓑ Gettysburg Address
Ⓒ Constitution   Ⓓ Pamphlet *Common Sense*

$x=y^2$
A bookstore owner buys a book for half off the retail price (n) and then sells it for 20% more than she bought it for. What does the bookstore owner sell the book for?

Compare the weight of your skin to the weight of your brain.
Ⓐ Same weight   Ⓑ Brain weighs twice as much
Ⓒ Skin weighs three times as much   Ⓓ Brain weighs ten times as much

Score: ___ / 7

Challenge 99

Objects that are dropped from a tall building or an airplane increase their speed as they fall. If you ignore the effect of air slowing the object down, by how much does the speed of the object increase each second?

- Ⓐ 7 mph
- Ⓑ 22 mph
- Ⓒ 39 mph
- Ⓓ 60 mph

A clerk at a bookstore wants to sell six books and average $20 per book sale. She sold five books at the following prices: $18, $18, $18, $16, $14.
What must she sell the sixth book for to average $20 per book?

A barometric pressure of 27.05 is:

- Ⓐ Impossible, it can never be that low
- Ⓑ Associated with category 5 hurricanes
- Ⓒ Associated with cool, clear weather
- Ⓓ Impossible, never that high

Name the four time zones in the continental United States.

"Four score and seven years ago" is the beginning of the Gettysburg Address. How many years is "Four score and seven years"?

- Ⓐ 407
- Ⓑ 47
- Ⓒ 87
- Ⓓ 67

If c computers cost n dollars, how much does one computer cost?

In the formula $E=mc^2$, the E stands for energy. What does the m and the c stand for?

Score: ___ / 7

Challenge 100

A flea 1/16th of an inch tall can jump 10 inches high. If a cat that is one foot tall could jump like a flea, how high could it jump?

What is the cost of carpet for a room that is 10 yards by 8 yards if the cost of carpet is $2 per square foot?

Winds can make cold temperatures feel even colder. Wind chill charts tell how cold it feels based on temperature and wind speed. If the temperature is 10° F and the wind speed is 40 mph, what is the wind chill?

Ⓐ 2° F   Ⓑ -5° F   Ⓒ -12° F   Ⓓ -37° F

The lowest mountain in the world is Mount Wycheproof (Australia) which has a summit _____ feet above the surrounding plains.

Ⓐ 12 feet   Ⓑ 140 feet   Ⓒ 1160 feet   Ⓓ 3212 feet

Abraham Lincoln had _____ year/years of formal schooling.

Ⓐ Less than one   Ⓑ Four   Ⓒ Eight   Ⓓ 13.5

What is the mean of 5 consecutive multiples of 5 when the smallest is n?

How many milligrams are in a kilogram?

Ⓐ 1000   Ⓑ 10,000   Ⓒ 100,000   Ⓓ 1,000,000

Score: ___ / 7

ANSWERS

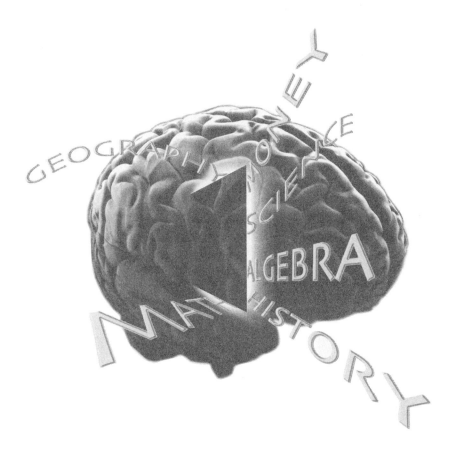

ANSWERS

Challenge 1

In the sequence 1,4,9,16,25, the 6th number is 36.
What is the 20th number?

400

Each number is squared. 8th number would be 64. 9th would be 81 and so forth.

A charge of .01 dollars per minute is how many times more expensive than .01 cents per minute?

100 times

.01 dollars is equal to one cent.   .01 cents is equal to 1/100 of a cent.

The smallest bone found in the human body is located in the middle ear. How long is it?

Ⓐ **1/10 of an inch**

What is the name of the world's smallest country? (Land mass)

Ⓓ **Vatican City**

Name one of the five years the Civil War was fought.

1861-1865

The value of *n* quarters expressed as cents is:

25*n* cents

*Each quarter has a value of 25 cents.
n quarters have a value of 25n cents.*

The first heart transplant was performed in 1967.
How long did the patient live?

Ⓑ **18 days**

ANSWERS

ANSWERS
Challenge 2

10^{10} is how many times larger than 10^6?

Ⓐ **10,000 times**

10,000,000,000 divided by 1,000,000 = 10,000

One million dollars is to one trillion dollars as one dollar is to:

Ⓓ **$1,000,000**

$$\frac{1{,}000{,}000}{1{,}000{,}000{,}000{,}000} = \frac{1}{1{,}000{,}000}$$

How many times does a heart beat in an average life?

Ⓒ **2,500,000,000**

60 beats per minute x 60 minutes in an hour x 24 hours in a day x 365 days in a year x 72 years = 2,270,592,000

The 2011 Tohoku earthquake off the eastern coast of Japan caused a tsunami at the Fukushima power plant with waves as high as:

Ⓐ **45 feet**

When was the airplane invented?

Ⓒ **1903**

Mary is 5 inches taller than Steve. If Steve is *n* inches tall, how tall is Mary?

(*n* + 5) inches

If Steve was 60 inches, Mary would be 60 + 5 = 65 inches
Steve is n inches, so Mary is (n+ 5) inches

The weight of a teaspoon of neutron star on earth is closest to the weight of:

Ⓓ **500,000,000 cars**

ANSWERS

ANSWERS

Challenge 3

What is the probability of rolling 2 of a kind when two dice are rolled?

Ⓐ **1/6**

Roll one die, then the second roll has a 1 in 6 probability of matching the first roll.

What did a gallon of milk cost in 1970?

Ⓑ **$1.15**

It takes sound approximately:

Ⓐ **5 seconds to go one mile**

Sound travels at a speed of 1100 feet per second. It takes sound approximately five seconds to travel the 5280 feet that are in a mile.

The tallest mountain on earth has an elevation of:

Ⓑ **5.5 miles**

Mount Everest has an elevation of 29035 feet. 29035 ÷ 5280 = 5.5 miles

In what time period was the steam locomotive invented?

Ⓑ **1780-1820**

A new building will be *n* feet high.
How many inches will the new building be?

12*n*

There are 12 inches in a foot, so the building's height in inches would be 12 times its height in feet.

How many ants are there for each person on earth?

Ⓒ **1,000,000**

ANSWERS

ANSWERS

Challenge 4

If you have 100 feet of fencing,
what shape will make a garden with the largest area?

Ⓐ **A circle**

If you had 50 billion dollars and spent one million dollars a day,
how long would your money last? (Round to nearest year)

137 years

50 billion ÷ 1 million = 50,000 days ÷ 365.25 days in a year = 136.89 years

Water boils at 212 degrees Fahrenheit at sea level.
At what temperature does water boil at the top of Mount Everest?

Ⓐ **154 degrees F**

Where does the United States
rank in life expectancy? (United Nations data)

Ⓓ **36th**

How many people have been president of the United States?

43

A bike tire does 2400 complete revolutions in a minute.
How many revolutions will it do in *n* seconds?

Ⓑ **40n**

The bike tire would do only 1/60 of the revolutions in one second.
1/60 x 2400 = 40 in one second   40 x n or 40n in n seconds

How tall was the tallest female on record?

Ⓒ **8 feet 1.75 inches**

Zeng Jinlian from China. Confirmed by Guinness World Records
as the tallest female ever.

ANSWERS

ANSWERS

Challenge 5

Stan has 1,000,000 dollars in base 2. How much money does he have in base 10?

Ⓐ **$64**

The columns in base 2 are:

128	64	32	16	8	4	2	1
	1	0	0	0	0	0	0

Stan has 1 group of 64 and zero groups of 32, 16, 8, 4, 2, 1

A United State's dollar converts to $1.25 of Canadian money. What does a dollar of Canadian money convert to in United State's dollars?

Ⓓ **$.80**

$$\frac{\$1(U.S.)}{\$1.25(Canadian)} = \frac{n}{\$1(Canadian)} \quad \$1.25n = 1 \quad 1 \div \$1.25 = \$.80$$

The speed of light is how many times faster than the speed of sound?

Ⓓ **1,000,000 times**

The speed of light is 186,000 miles per second.
Sound takes 5 seconds to go one mile, so it travels 1/5 of a mile in one second.
186,000 ÷ 1/5 = 930,000

Water covers _____ of the earth.

Ⓒ **70%**

Name one of the five years the first World War was fought.

1914-1918

Sara spent $190 for two presents.
If the first present cost *n* dollars, how much did the second one cost?

$190 - *n*

Total is $190. If you spend *n*, the remaining amount is $190 - *n*.

What was the national debt for the United States on December 12th 2011 at 10:30 Central Time?

Ⓒ **$15,107,645,000,000**

ANSWERS

ANSWERS

Challenge 6

.25% is equal to:

Ⓓ **1/400**

.25% is a quarter of 1%   *1% is 1/100*   *1/4 of 1/100 = 1/400*

Students graduating from college in 2011 who took out loans to fund their college education had an average student loan debt of:

Ⓒ **$25,000**

A blue whale's weight can be as high as _____ pounds.

Ⓑ **300,000 pounds**

How high would the sea level rise if all of Antarctica's ice sheets melted?

Ⓓ **200 feet**

Name the two presidents who were in office during World War II.

Roosevelt and Truman

My grandfather's age is 5 times my age. My father's age is three times my age and my sister is three years younger than I am. If I am *n* years old, what is the combined age of all four of us?

10*n* - 3

Grandfather's age: 5n
Father's age: 3n
Sister's age: n-3
All ages: 5n + 3n + n - 3 + n = 10n - 3

The tallest tree ever discovered was:

Ⓐ **A 435 foot Australian eucalyptus**

ANSWERS

ANSWERS

Challenge 7

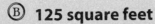

If the perimeter of a rectangle is 60 feet and one of the sides is equal to 5 feet, then the area of the rectangle must be:

Ⓑ **125 square feet**

The two widths total 5 + 5 = 10   The lengths then total 60 - 10 = 50
Each length must equal 25 feet   5 x 25 = 125 square feet

Financial experts advise college students to limit their student loans to:

Ⓐ **One year's salary for the field they are entering**

How many typical viruses would it take to circle a quarter?

Ⓒ **500,000**

What is the name of the only Great Lake that does not border Canada?

Lake Michigan

When was World War II fought?

Ⓑ **1939-1945**

There are six horses and *n* ducks on a farm.
How many legs are there altogether?

24 + 2n

24 horse legs and 2n duck legs   Total: 24 + 2n

How much gold is in a cubic mile of sea water? (Weight)

Ⓓ **25 - 100 pounds**

ANSWERS

ANSWERS
Challenge 8

How long would it take light to travel around the equator of the earth?

Ⓑ **1/7 of a second**

The equator is 25,000 miles around.
Light travels at a speed of 186,000 miles per second.
186,000 ÷ 25,000 = .13 seconds

A home mortgage for a $100,000 loan at an interest rate of 3% would call for a monthly payment of $421.60. If the interest rate was 14%, what would the monthly payment be?

Ⓒ **$1184.87**   (check online mortgage calculator)

The lowest possible temperature expressed in Fahrenheit is:

Ⓑ **-459.67° F**

What percent of the world's fresh water is held in the ice of Antarctica?

Ⓑ **70 %**

Name two of the three main countries that the United States was at war with during World War II.

Germany, Japan, and Italy

How many millimeters are in n meters?

1000n

There are 1000 millimeters in each meter.

How many people die worldwide each year of smoking related causes?

Ⓒ **5 million**

ANSWERS

ANSWERS

Challenge 9

The circumference of a circle divided by the radius is equal to:

Ⓑ 2π

Circumference = π x Diameter or Circumference = π x 2 x radius
Circumference ÷ radius = 2π

The current national debt (2011) is over 15 trillion dollars. What was the national debt in 1970?

Ⓐ **381 billion dollars**

What is closest in size to a blue whale's heart?

Ⓓ **Car**

Where does the United States rank in the list of most populated countries?

Ⓐ **3rd**

The Declaration of Independence was signed in 1776. In what year did George Washington take office as president of the United States?

Ⓓ **1789**

How many hours are there in *n* seconds?

n/3600

A second is 1/60 of a minute. A second is 1/3600 of an hour.

A liter of water weighs:

Ⓒ **Exactly 1 kilogram**

ANSWERS

ANSWERS

Challenge 10

A meter is to a nanometer as the earth is to:

Ⓑ **Marble**

A nanometer is 1,000,000,000th of a meter.
Earth's diameter is 8000 miles x 5280 feet x 12 inches = 506,880,000 inches
A marble has an approximate diameter of 1/2 inch.

A gallon of gas cost _____ in 1970.

Ⓐ **36 cents**

How far away is the closest star to earth? (excluding our sun)

Ⓐ **4.2 light years**

The longest river in the world is:

Ⓐ **The Nile**

4130 miles

How many Supreme Court justices are there?

9 justices

What is the sum of five consecutive numbers?
(The smallest is *n*)

5*n* +10

Smallest: n   Next: n+1   Next: n+2   Next: n+3   Next: n+4
Added together: 5n +10

A normal birth weight is 7-8 pounds. In 2004,
the world's tiniest baby was born.
How much did she weigh at birth? (She is healthy today.)

Ⓐ **9.2 ounces**

ANSWERS

ANSWERS

Challenge 11

A speed of 60 miles per hour
is the same as _____ kilometers per hour.

96.6 kph (96 or 97 would be correct)

1 miles = 1.61 kilometers   60 miles x 1.61 = 96.6 kilometers per hour

What was the average price of a new home in 1960?

Ⓐ **$12,700**

The fastest land animal is the cheetah (65 mph). The slowest land animal is the three-toed sloth. What is the top speed of the three-toed sloth?

Ⓑ **.15 miles per hour**

There are only two states that have
not had the temperature reach 100° F.
Alaska is one, what is the other state?

Hawaii

What are the three branches of government in the United States?

Legislative, executive and judicial

What is the sum of five consecutive even numbers?
(The smallest is *n*)

5*n* + 20

n + (*n*+2) + (*n*+4) + (*n*+6) + (*n*+8) = 5*n* + 20

On average, how many lightning bolts hit the earth each second?

Ⓐ **100**

ANSWERS

ANSWERS
Challenge 12

What is the next number?
0, 1, 1, 2, 3, 5, 8, 13, 21, 34, 55, ?

89

Each number is the sum of the preceding two numbers.

A book that cost $80 on Monday is discounted 50% on Tuesday; another 50% on Wednesday and so forth (an additional 50% each day). What will the cost of the book be on Sunday?

$1.25

.5 of $80 = $40 on Tuesday
.5 of $40 = $20 on Wednesday
.5 of $20 = $10 on Thursday
.5 of $10 = $5 on Friday
.5 of $5 = $2.50 on Saturday
.5 of $2.50 = $1.25 on Sunday

The loudest animal is the blue whale. Keeping in mind that a whisper is 30 decibels and a jet engine 140 decibels, how many decibels are the sounds of a blue whale?

Ⓒ **185 decibels**

The amount of ice in the Antarctic is what fraction of the amount of water in the Atlantic?

Ⓑ **1/10**

In what year was the attack by the Japanese on Pearl Harbor?

1941

If the circumference of a circle is *n*, what is the diameter?

n/π   *Diameter x π = n   (Circumference)*
Divide both sides by π   Diameter = n/π

How many pounds of food does the average person eat in a lifetime?

Ⓒ **60,000 pounds**

ANSWERS

ANSWERS

Challenge 13

If five barrels each have five cats, who each have five kittens, how many total legs are there?

600 legs

Each barrel has 5 adult cats and 25 kittens = 30 x 4 = 120 legs
120 legs x 5 barrels = 600 legs

The price of a gallon of milk increased from $8 to $10. What was the percent of increase?

25%

Percent of increase is found by dividing the amount of increase by the original price: 2 ÷ 8 = .25 or 25%

The smallest rodent is the pigmy jerboa which weighs approximately 1/4 of an ounce. The largest rodent is a capybara. It can weigh as much as_____.

Ⓓ **150 pounds**

What country is closest to the United States? (Not including Canada and Mexico)

Ⓐ **Russia**

Who was president during the Civil War, World War I, and the beginning of the Korean War?

Abraham Lincoln, Woodrow Wilson, Harry Truman

The width of a rectangle is called *n*.
If the length of a rectangle is 8 times the width, what is the perimeter?

18n

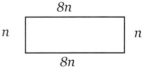

For every person who is killed by a shark, _____ sharks are killed by humans.

Ⓒ **5-10 million**

ANSWERS

ANSWERS
Challenge 14

Rat A swam across the middle of a lake with a one mile diameter. Rat B walked around the lake to the other side to meet Rat A. How much farther did Rat B travel?

.57 miles

Rat A traveled one mile. Rat B traveled half the circumference of a circle with a one mile diameter.

Circumference = πD or 3.14

Rat B walked halfway around the circle: 3.14 ÷ 2 = 1.57 --> 1.57 - 1 = .57

A person who has a net worth of 50 billion dollars gave one million dollars to charity. How much must a person who has a net worth of $1000 give to charity to give away the same fraction of his wealth as the billionaire?

Ⓐ **2 cents**

$\dfrac{1{,}000{,}000}{50{,}000{,}000{,}000}$ reduces to $\dfrac{1}{50{,}000}$ $\dfrac{1}{50{,}000}$ x $1000 = $.02 or 2 cents

Galapagos tortoises can weigh as much as 500 pounds. What is their life span?

Ⓑ **150 years**

There is enough salt in all five oceans to cover all the continents to a depth of nearly _____ feet.

Ⓒ **500 feet**

The shortest war on record was fought between Zanzibar and England in 1896. Zanzibar surrendered after 38 _____.

Ⓑ **Minutes**

Bill received a 25% raise in 2011. If his original salary is *n*, what is his new salary?

1.25*n*

.25 of n = .25n raise   Salary: n + raise of .25n = 1.25n

How long can human tapeworms grow?

Ⓐ **70 feet**

ANSWERS

ANSWERS
Challenge 15

The amount of time it takes for a spacecraft to travel to Mars is _____ times the amount of time it takes for a spacecraft to travel to the Moon.

 85

It takes approximately 3 days to travel to the Moon and 250 days to Mars.

People with an excellent credit rating are often able to acquire car loans with a 0% interest. If their credit rating is poor, they often must pay an interest rate of 16%. A 5-year $24,000 car loan at 0% interest has a monthly payment of $400. What is the monthly payment if the interest rate is 16%?

© **$583.63**

(Use an online car loan calculator)
The best way to estimate a car payment is to cut the time of the loan in half: 2.5
Multiply the 2.5 times the interest rate: 2.5 x 16% = 40%
Interest paid: 40% of $24,000 = $9600   Total cost of car: $9600 + 24,000 = $33,600
divided by 60 months (5-year loan) = $560

The fastest flier in the animal kingdom is the peregrine falcon. How fast can it fly?

© **185 miles per hour**

What is the northern most state of the lower 48 states?
Minnesota

The Tunguska explosion was a powerful explosion that occurred in Russia in 1908. The explosion is thought to have been caused by an exploding large meteoroid or comet fragment at an altitude of several miles above the earth's surface. The power of the Tunguska explosion is thought to have been:

© **1,000 times more powerful than the atomic bomb dropped on Hiroshima, Japan**

Sales tax in a state is 7%.
If the cost of a computer without tax is n dollars, what is the amount of sales tax?

.07n   7% of n = .07 x n or .07n

The largest recorded tsunami was caused by a landslide in Lituya Bay, Alaska in 1958. How many feet high was it?

Ⓓ **1720 feet**

ANSWERS

ANSWERS
Challenge 16

The first 5 prime numbers are:

Ⓐ **2, 3, 5, 7, 11**

Bill's 2009 salary of $100,000 was cut by 50% in 2010. He was then given a 50% raise in 2011. What was his 2011 salary?

Ⓑ **$75,000**

2010 salary: $50,000   2011 salary: 50% raise = .50 x $50,000 = $25,000

An African black mamba snake releases enough venom in one bite to kill _____ humans.

Ⓓ **Over 10**

The largest desert in the world is the Sahara Desert. Its area is:

Ⓓ **About the same size as the United States**

In what year was the most famous San Francisco Earthquake?

Ⓑ **1906**

Sales tax is 5%. A computer is on sale for 30% off the original price. If the original price is n, what is the new price for the computer including tax?

.735n

Discount: .3 x n = .3n   New price: n - .3n = .7n
Tax: .05 x .7n = .035n   .7n (price) + .035n (tax) = .735n

There are more _____ in United State's households kept as pets than any other animal.

Ⓒ **Fish**

ANSWERS

ANSWERS

Challenge 17

1.1 in base 2 is equal to what number in base 10?

Ⓒ **1.5**

Base 2 columns: 64 32 16 8 4 2 1 . 1/2 1/4 1/8
                                                          1   1

One group of 1 and one group of 1/2: 1 + 1/2 = 1.5

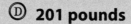

When buying a house, a good rule is to keep your monthly mortgage payment, including principal, interest, real estate taxes and homeowner's insurance, under _____ of your gross monthly income.

Ⓑ **28%**

If a person weighed 200 pounds at the equator, how much would he weigh at the poles?

Ⓓ **201 pounds**

You weigh more at the poles because you are closer to the earth's center of gravity.

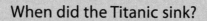

The largest recorded earthquake was the Great Chilean Earthquake of May 22, 1960 with a magnitude of:

Ⓑ **9.5**

When did the Titanic sink?

Ⓒ **1912**

Angle B is 3 times larger than angle A, which we will call n. What is the size of angle C?

Angle C: 180 - 4n
Angle A: n
Angle B: 3n

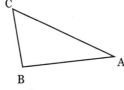

(Total angles in a triangle add up to 180 degrees.)

Ants are capable of carrying objects _____ times their body weight.

Ⓓ **50**

ANSWERS

ANSWERS

Challenge 18

Sales tax on an item is $22.50. If the tax rate is 7.5%, what was the cost of the item before tax?

$300

7.5% of something is equal to $22.50
.075 x n = $22.50 $22.50 ÷ .075 = $300

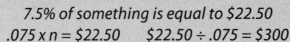

A ballot measure in Arizona called for an 80 cent tax on a pack of cigarettes. The ballot language called for a .80 cent increase. How much money per pack does this ballot language call for?

Ⓓ **8/10 of a cent**

.80 dollars is 80 cents   .80 cents is 8/10 of a cent

Pound for pound, what is the strongest muscle in the body?

Ⓒ **Tongue**

What is the smallest of the five oceans?

Ⓐ **Arctic**

Which president was in office at the time of the Louisiana Purchase?

Thomas Jefferson

Thomas Jefferson proposed and completed the Louisiana Purchase from France and Napoleon in 1803.

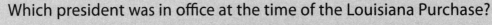

There are nickels and dimes in a jar. If there are 20 total coins in the jar and you call the number of nickels *n*, what is the value of the coins in the jar expressed as cents?

200 - 5*n*

Number of nickels: n   Value of nickels: 5n
Number of dimes: 20 - n   Value of the dimes: 10(20 - n) or 200 - 10n
5n + 200 - 10n = 200 - 5n

What was the name of the machine that was used by Nazi Germany for the encryption and decryption of secret messages during World War II?

Enigma

ANSWERS

ANSWERS

Challenge 19

A gold coin with a diameter of 11.6 millimeters is closest in size to which of the following:

Ⓒ **Aspirin**

1 millimeter = 0.039 inches   11.6 x .039 = .45 inches

The cost of a computer after a 20% discount is $600. What is the regular cost of the computer?

Ⓐ **$750**

80% of something = $600

(A 20% discount means the computer cost 80% of the original price.)

.8 x n = $600   n = $600 ÷ .8 = $750

Even though your brain is only 2% of your total body weight, it requires _____ percent of the oxygen and calories your body needs.

Ⓐ **20%**

What percent of the world's population lives in China?

Ⓐ **19%**

The purchase of Alaska from Russia was called Seward's Folly. Who was the U.S. president at the time of the acquisition?

Andrew Johnson

In a box of change, there are twice as many dimes as nickels and twice as many quarters as dimes. If nickels are called *n*, what is the value of the coins in the box expressed as cents?

125*n*

Nickels: n	*Value: 5n*	
Dimes: 2n	*Value: 20n*	
Quarters: 4n	*Value: 100n*	100n + 20n + 5n = 125n

How old was the oldest living animal?

Ⓓ **405 years old** (Ming the clam)

ANSWERS

ANSWERS

Challenge 20

How long would it take sound to travel around the equator of the earth?

Ⓒ **34.7 hours**

Sound travels one mile in 5 seconds.
There are 25,000 miles around the equator, so sound takes:
25,000 x 5 = 125,000 seconds
125,000 seconds ÷ 3600 seconds in an hour = 34.7 hours

If a 20 year old deposits $100 in a savings account at 2% annual interest, approximately how much money will the $100 have grown to when he is 60 years old?

Ⓐ **$200**

A good rule for determining growth of money is to divide 72 by the interest rate. Your answer will give you an approximate number of years before money will double.
72 ÷ 2 = 36   Money will double in 36 years.

The weight of the world's largest giant sequoia (General Sherman) is _____ pounds.

Ⓒ **2,500,000**

What is the northern most, eastern most, and western most state in the United States?

Ⓒ **Alaska, Alaska, Alaska**

Name the two pairs of father-son presidents.
(The 4th and the 6th as well as the 41st and the 43rd)

1) John Adams & John Q Adams   2) George HW Bush & George W Bush

Eric is half his father's height. Eric's pet dog is half Eric's height and also twice the height of Eric's pet cat. Eric's hamster is 1/4 the height of the cat. If the hamster is n inches tall, how tall is Eric's dad?

32n

Hamster: n Cat: $4n$ Dog: $8n$ Eric: $16n$ Father: $32n$

The giant sequoia is the world's most massive living thing. The largest giant sequoia, named General Sherman, has a circumference at the base of _____ feet.

Ⓓ **100**

ANSWERS

ANSWERS

Challenge 21

How long does it take light from the sun to reach the earth?

8 minutes and 20 seconds

93,000,000 ÷ 186,000 miles per second = 500 seconds   8 minutes 20 seconds

You borrow $500 from a bank for a computer.
If the annual interest rate is 5% and you pay the minimum monthly payment of $15, how long will it take to pay off the loan?

Ⓑ **3 years**

How many miles of blood vessels are in the human body?

Ⓒ **60,000 miles**

The name and population of the world's most populous metropolitan area is:

Ⓐ **Tokyo with 33,000,000 people**

Name 11 of the original 13 colonies:

Connecticut	**Delaware**	**Georgia**
Maryland	**Massachusetts**	**New Hampshire**
New Jersey	**New York**	**North Carolina**
Pennsylvania	**Rhode Island**	**South Carolina** **Virginia**

The perimeter of a rectangle is 7 times the width.
If the width is n, what is the length of the rectangle?

2.5n

Width: n Perimeter: $7n$ $n + n + 2\ lengths = 7n$
2 lengths = $5n$ length = $2.5n$

A rain drop will always break into smaller drops when it reaches its maximum speed. A rain drop's top speed is:

Ⓐ **18 mph**

ANSWERS

ANSWERS

Challenge 22

Usain Bolt holds the world record for the 100 meter sprint at 9.58 seconds. How many miles per hour is this speed?

Ⓐ **23.3 miles per hour**

1000 meters (kilometer) = .62 miles, so .062 miles are in 100 meters

$$\frac{9.58 \text{ (seconds)}}{.062 \text{ (miles)}} = \frac{3600 \text{ (seconds in hour)}}{n}$$

$9.58n = 223.2 \qquad n = 23.3$

If a 20 year old deposits $100 in a savings account at 12% annual interest, approximately how much money will the $100 have grown to when he is 60 years old?

Ⓑ **$12,000**

Divide 72 by the interest rate to find the number of years until money doubles:
$72 \div 12 = 6$ *Every 6 years the money will double.*

How far is Mars from the Sun?

Ⓒ **130,000,000 miles**

It has recently been discovered that Florida and the Hudson Bay are getting _____ closer every year. (Distance)

Ⓐ **2/3 of a millimeter**

What amendment gave women the right to vote?

19th

A pie is divided into *n* equal pieces and 6 are then eaten. What fraction of the pie is left?

Ⓓ **(n-6) ÷ n**

If the pie was broken into 8 pieces: (8-6) ÷ 8

A typical American car can travel 25 miles per gallon of gas. How many miles will a 747 jet travel for each gallon of jet fuel?

Ⓒ **1/5 of a mile**

ANSWERS

ANSWERS

Challenge 23

A googol is defined as a one followed by how many zeros?

Ⓐ **100**

If you have a student loan of $250,000 at 8% interest, how much will you pay each month for the 20 years it takes to pay off the loan?

Ⓒ **$2100**

(Check internet mortgage calculator)

How many electrons are in an atom of uranium?

Ⓑ **92**

What is the name of the world's largest country? (Land mass)

Ⓑ **Russia**

The amendment that gave women the right to vote was ratified in:

Ⓒ **1920**

Alicia traveled *n* hours at 60 miles per hour.
How many miles has she traveled?

60*n*

At 60 mph, you travel at one mile each minute, or 60 miles each hour.

How many people are killed each year in the United States by lightning, sharks, bees and dogs?

Ⓐ **Lightning 58; Sharks .5; Bees 50; Dogs 30**

ANSWERS

ANSWERS

Challenge 24

$8^0 + 8^0 + 1^0$ is equal to:

Ⓓ **3**

Numbers to the "0" power are equal to one.

If you have a student loan of $250,000 at 3% interest, how much will you pay each month for the 20 years it takes to pay off the loan?

Ⓓ **$1400**

(Check internet mortgage calculator)

What is the temperature at the center of the sun?

Ⓒ **27,000,000 degrees Fahrenheit**

The longest name for a village is in Wales. How many letters does it have?

Ⓐ **59 letters**

Llanfairpwllgwyngyllgogerychwyrndrobwyll llantysiliogogogoch

How long was the Lewis and Clark expedition?

Ⓓ **2 years 4 months**

Natalie is going on a 900 mile trip. So far, she has traveled *n* hours at 60 miles per hour. How many miles of her trip does she have remaining?

900 - 60n

*Because she is traveling at 60 mph, her distance will be 60 miles each hour, or 60n.
Total distance - amount traveled: 900 - 60n*

What percent of the world's population used the internet in 2011?

Ⓑ **25%**

ANSWERS

ANSWERS

Challenge 25

What is the probability of rolling three of the same number when you roll three dice?

Ⓑ 1/36

*First roll does not matter.
The probability of the second die matching the first is 1/6.
The probability of the third die matching the first two is 1/6.   1/1 x 1/6 x 1/6 = 1/36*

"Rent to own" companies usually end up charging consumers _____ the cost of the item.

Ⓑ 3 to 4 times

The distance from the Earth to Mars, when they are at their closest, is _____ times the distance from the Earth to the Moon at their closest.

Ⓑ 150

Put these places in order from west to east: Anchorage, Hawaii, Tahiti.

Ⓓ Hawaii, Anchorage, Tahiti

The treaty between Great Britain and the United States that gave recognition to the existence of the United States was:

Ⓐ Treaty of Paris

Each week Daniel is paid $8.50 per hour plus a bonus of $50. How much did he earn in a week where he worked n hours?

Ⓐ 8.50n$ + $50

His pay is 8.50n$ + bonus: 8.50n$ + $50

How long can a sperm whale hold its breath?

Ⓐ 2 hours

ANSWERS

ANSWERS

Challenge 26

What is the next number in the following list of numbers? 1, 8, 27, 64, ?

Ⓒ **125**

Each number is a cube: 1^3, 2^3, 3^3 etc.

In what year was the price of a first class stamp 6 cents?

Ⓓ **1970**

How much would a 200 pound person weigh on the moon?

Ⓐ **33 pounds**

Weight on the moon is 16.5% of weight on Earth.

The country with the longest life expectancy for a female is Japan at _____ years old. (United Nations data)

Ⓒ **86.1**

What was the primary event/events which led to the United States entering World War I?

Germans sinking U.S. ships with submarines

This bread is *n* minutes old. How old is the bread expressed in days?

Ⓓ **n/1440**

n minutes old = $\frac{n}{60}$ hours = $\frac{n}{60} \div 24$ days = $\frac{n}{60} \times \frac{1}{24} = \frac{n}{1440}$ days

Which state had the most deaths caused by lightning from 2001-2010?

Florida

ANSWERS

ANSWERS

Challenge 27

How many cubic inches are in a cubic foot?

Ⓒ **1728**

12 x 12 = 144 square inches in a square foot
144 x 12 = 1728 cubic inches in a cubic foot

Total outstanding student loan debt for the United States in 2011 was:

Ⓐ **950 billion dollars**

The diameter of the sun is approximately
how many times larger than the diameter of the earth?

Ⓐ **100**

The diameter of the earth is 8000 miles.
The diameter of the sun is 865,000 miles.   865,000 ÷ 8000 = 108.125

Hawaii is moving toward Japan at a rate of _____ per year.

Ⓑ **4 inches**

What was the name of the first man-made satellite?

Sputnik

If you can throw a baseball *n* feet,
how many miles can you throw a baseball?

n/5280

Because there are 5280 feet in a mile, there are n ÷ 5280 miles in n feet

Robert Wadlow is considered to be the tallest person in history.
How tall was he?

Ⓐ **8 feet 11.1 inches**

ANSWERS

ANSWERS

Challenge 28

In a box containing red and blue marbles, 30 marbles are picked at random and the result is 12 red and 18 blue marbles. After the 30 marbles are replaced, the box contains a total of 1000 marbles. How many red marbles would you estimate are in the box?

Ⓒ **400**

In every group of 30 marbles, you would expect 12 red marbles.
There are 1000 ÷ 30 = 33.3 groups of 30 marbles in a box of 1000 marbles.
33.3 x 12 = 400

If you have a credit card balance of $50,000 at 34.9% interest, how much will you pay each month for the 5 years it takes to pay off the loan?

Ⓓ **$1800**

(Check internet mortgage calculator)

Approximately how many stars are in the universe?

Ⓑ **10^{23}**

The longest bridge in the United States is the Lake Pontchartrain Causeway. How long is it?

Ⓒ **23.9 miles**

Which president started a relationship with China?

Ⓑ **Nixon**

If a farm has *n* cows, 10 pigs and one duck, how many legs are on the farm?

4*n* + 42

n cows have 4*n* legs
10 pigs have 40 legs and one duck has 2 legs = 4*n* + 42

What is the probability of being bitten by a dog in the United States in a given year?

Ⓐ **1/50**

ANSWERS

ANSWERS

Challenge 29

What is the lowest common denominator for
1/2, 1/3, 1/4, 1/5, and 1/6?

Ⓑ **60**

What does it cost to raise a medium-size dog to the age of eleven?

Ⓓ **$16,400**

How hot is lightning?

Ⓒ **6 times hotter than the surface of the sun**

The wettest place on earth is
Mawsynram, Meghalaya (India) with _____ of rainfall each year.

Ⓑ **467 inches**

The _____ Doctrine said that European countries
should not try to gain influence in the Western Hemisphere.

Monroe

Solve for n: $1/2n - 4 = 20$

$n = 48$

$1/2n = 24 \quad n = 48$

Pick the true statement about the rate of infant eye blinking.

Ⓒ **Infants blink 1 or 2 times each minute**

ANSWERS

ANSWERS

Challenge 30

$6 + 4 \div 2 \times 0 =$

Ⓐ **6**

Order of operations
$4 \div 2 = 2 \times 0 = 0 + 6 = 6$

What is .50% of $500?

$2.50

.50% is 1/2 of one percent

The animal responsible for the most human deaths worldwide is the _____.

Ⓐ **mosquito**

The highest waterfall on earth is Angel Falls in Venezuela. How high is it?

Ⓓ **2648 feet**

Which presidents served during the Great Depression?

Hoover and Franklin Roosevelt

There are 35 total animals on a farm. If there are only goats and ducks and we call the number of ducks *n*, how many goats are there?

35 - *n*

A cubic foot of water weighs 62.4 pounds. What does a cubic foot of gold weigh?

Ⓐ **1206 pounds**

ANSWERS

ANSWERS

Challenge 31

What is closest to the value of pi?

Ⓒ **The ratio of the circumference of a circle to the diameter**

The definition of pi is the "ratio of the circumference of a circle to the diameter".

The Dow-Jones Industrial Average is near 12,000 today (2011).
What was the lowest level for the Dow-Jones in 1970?

Ⓑ **$669**

Pterodactyls had wingspans as wide as _____ feet.

Ⓓ **40 feet**

What is the mean income and median income of the 7 billion world population?

Ⓒ **$1700 and $7000**

When the world's income is divided by 7 billion,
the result is approximately $7000. (mean)
When the median (middle income) is determined, the results are very different.
Only 19% of the world's population live in countries where the per capita
income is above $7000.

The Emancipation Proclamation:

Ⓐ **Freed the slaves**

The distance around a circular pool is *n* meters.
What is the distance in centimeters?

100*n* centimeters

There are 100 centimeters in a meter.

What is the exact length of a day? *(to the nearest second)*

23 hours 56 minutes 4 seconds

ANSWERS

ANSWERS

Challenge 32

If you hear thunder 20 seconds after there is a lightning strike, the storm is how many miles away?

Ⓓ 4 miles

*It takes sound 5 seconds to travel one mile.
The thunder and lightning occur at the same time.
The thunder takes 20 seconds to reach your ears: 20 ÷ 5 = 4 miles away.*

In what year was the price of eggs 91 cents?

Ⓒ 1980

How fast does sound travel in water?

Ⓐ 4 - 5 times faster than air

The coldest temperature recorded on earth was in Vostok, Antarctica. What was the temperature?

Ⓒ -128.6° F

When was the United Nations formed?

Ⓑ After World War II

What is the average of five consecutive numbers where the smallest number is *n*?

$n + 2$

Add all five numbers and then divide by 5.
$n + (n+1) + (n+2) + (n+3) + (n+4) = 5n + 10$

$$\frac{5n + 10}{5} = \frac{5(n+2)}{5} = n + 2$$

How many gallons of jet fuel does a fully loaded 747 use when it travels from Boston to Los Angeles?

Ⓑ 15,000 gallons

ANSWERS

ANSWERS

Challenge 33

What is the result when you take
1/2 of 1/25 and then square 1/2 of that answer?

Ⓐ **1/10,000**

1/2 x 1/25 = 1/50 x 1/2 = 1/100
1/100 x 1/100 = 1/10,000

How much does it cost to pay for the electricity if a
250-watt incandescent bulb is on for 24 hours and electricity
cost 10 cents per kilowatt hour?

60 cents

How many grains of sand are there on the earth?

Ⓐ **10^{21}**

The hottest temperature recorded on earth was in El Azizia, Libya.
What was the temperature?

Ⓐ **136° F**

When was the League of Nations formed?

Ⓒ **After World War I**

The distance across (diameter) a circular pool is *n* meters.
What is the circumference in decimeters?

31.4*n*

*3.14 x n is the circumference in meters.
Because there are 10 decimeters in each meter, the answer is 10 x 3.14n = 31.4n*

Chandra Bahadur Dangi is considered to be the shortest person on record.
How tall is he?

Ⓒ **21.5 inches**

ANSWERS

ANSWERS

Challenge 34

What is the probability of flipping a coin and getting 10 heads in a row?

Ⓑ Approximately 1 in 1000

There is a 1/2 probability of a head each flip.

$$\frac{1}{2} \times \frac{1}{2} \times \frac{1}{2} \times \frac{1}{2} \times \frac{1}{2} \times \frac{1}{2} \times \frac{1}{2} \times \frac{1}{2} \times \frac{1}{2} \times \frac{1}{2} = \frac{1}{1024}$$

What is .01% of $100?

One cent

How long does it take for light to travel from the center of the sun to the surface?

Ⓓ 100,000 to 200,000 years

What percent of the world's population lives in the Northern Hemisphere?

Ⓓ 90%

When was Social Security established?

Ⓒ 1935

If there are *n* quarts of water in a bathtub, how many gallons are there in the tub?

n/4

What percent of the world's population is male?

Ⓓ 50.4%

ANSWERS

ANSWERS

Challenge 35

A cubic millimeter is what fraction of a cubic meter?

Ⓒ **1/1,000,000,000**

*There are 1000 millimeters in a meter.
A cubic meter is 1000 millimeters on each side.
1000 x 1000 x 1000 = 1,000,000,000 cubic millimeters in a cubic meter.*

**The price of a gallon of milk decreased from $10 to $8.
What was the percent of decrease?**

20%

*Percent of decrease is the amount of change over the original amount.
$2 divided by $10 = 20%*

How many earths would fit inside the sun?

Ⓐ **1,300,000**

**Since its formation some 12,000 years ago,
how far has Niagara Falls withdrawn upstream?**

Ⓓ **7 miles**

When was Medicare established?

Ⓓ **1965**

Jim ate .3475 of *n* pies. How many pies are left?

.6525*n* pies

**How many people in the United States
die of smoking related causes each year?**

Ⓑ **438,000**

ANSWERS

ANSWERS

Challenge 36

The distance from the earth to the moon is what fraction of the distance of the earth to the sun?

Ⓓ **1/400**

250,000 miles compared to 93,000,000 miles = 25/9300

How many billionaires are there in the world?

Ⓑ **1000**

Approximately how many stars are in our galaxy? (Milky Way)

Ⓓ **200,000,000,000**

Sea water has a salt content of roughly 3.5%. The Dead Sea has a salt content of ____ percent.

Ⓑ **30%**

Which president was known for saying the phrase: "Speak softly, but carry a big stick."?

Ⓐ **Theodore Roosevelt**

A bat and ball together cost $10. If the bat cost $9 more than the ball, what is the cost of the ball?

50 cents

Ball: n Bat: $n + 9$

Equation: $2n + 9 = 10$ $2n = 1$ $n = .5$ or 50 cents

What is the median age of the population of the United States?

Ⓓ **37 years old**

ANSWERS

ANSWERS

Challenge 37

You are given a penny on December 1st, 2 pennies on the 2nd, 4 pennies on the 3rd, 8 on the 4th, 16 on the 5th and so forth. How much money will you be given on December 31? (Express your answer in dollars.)

$10,737,418.24

December 1st you have: 2^0 or one cent

December 2nd you have: 2^1 or 2 cents

December 2nd you have: 2^2 or 4 cents

December 31st you have: 2^{30} or 1,073,741,824 cents or $10,737,418.24

What saving's interest rate would be needed to double $100 in 5 years?

Ⓒ **14%**

Divide 72 by number of years to get the doubling interest rate: 72/5 = 14.4

How fast does the earth spin?

Ⓒ **1000 mph**

The world's highest waterfall is how many times higher than Niagara Falls?

Ⓐ **15 times**

In what year was an atomic bomb dropped on Hiroshima?

Ⓒ **1945**

How many 8 foot sections of fencing are needed for a garden with a length that is 4 times its width? (Call width *n*)

1.25n

Width: *n*   Length: 4*n*

Perimeter: 10*n*   Fencing pieces needed: 10*n*/8 or 1.25 *n*

What is the golden ratio?

Ⓓ **1.62**

ANSWERS

ANSWERS

Challenge 38

How many different ways are there to hang four paintings on four hooks?

Ⓑ 24

Which is more expensive,
89 cents a square foot or $5 a square yard?

89 cents a square foot

There are 9 square feet in a square yard: $.89 x 9 = $8.01

At what temperature are Fahrenheit and Celsius the same number?

-40
C = (5/9) x (F-32)
*When temperatures are the same,
then we can replace the C in the equation with an F.*
F = (5/9) x (F-32)   Solve for F: F = -40°

Israel's Dead Sea's surface is _____ feet below sea level.

Ⓓ 1320

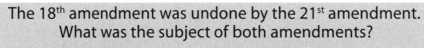

The 18th amendment was undone by the 21st amendment.
What was the subject of both amendments?

**The 18th amendment prohibited the manufacture, sale,
or transportation of intoxicating liquors within, the importation
thereof into, or the exportation thereof from the United States and
all territory subject to the jurisdiction thereof for beverage purposes.
Repealed by amendment 21.**

There are 35 total animals on a farm. If there are only goats and ducks and we call the number of ducks *n*, how many goats legs are there?

4(35 - *n*)

Ducks: *n*   Goats: 35 - *n*   Goat legs: 4(35 - *n*)

How deep can a sperm whale dive?

Ⓑ **5000-10,000 feet**

ANSWERS

ANSWERS

Challenge 39

One two-digit number is a perfect square and a perfect cube.
What is it?

64

8 x 8 = 64   4 x 4 x 4 = 64

The annual salary for the
President of the United States + the annual salary of the Vice-President
+ the salary of the Chief Justice of the U.S. Supreme Court =

Ⓐ **$854,200**

President: $400,000   Vice President: 230,700   Supreme Court: $223,500

What is the temperature on the surface of the sun?

Ⓐ **10,000 degrees Fahrenheit**

How long is the longest river in the world?

Ⓐ **4180 miles**

Which amendment states that any person born in the
United States is a citizen of the United States?

14th Amendment

If it takes *n* seconds to paint a wall,
how many hours does it take to paint the wall?

Ⓒ ***n* ÷ 3600**

How tall was Napoleon?

Ⓒ **5 feet 6.5 inches**

ANSWERS

ANSWERS

Challenge 40

A watch with an hour hand and a minute hand gains 16 minutes every day. Every _____ days, this broken watch will show the correct time.

Ⓑ 45 days

How many 16 minute segments until it reads 12 hours fast or 720 minutes fast?
720 ÷ 16 = 45 days

The annual salary for the president of the United States in 1789 was:

Ⓒ $25,000

Argentinosaurus is currently thought to have been the biggest dinosaur. What is it estimated to have weighed?

Ⓒ 100 tons

The deepest part of the ocean is called the Mariana Trench. What is its depth?

Ⓐ 6.75 miles

"We the people of the United States" is the beginning of:

Ⓓ Constitution

My grandfather's age is 5 times my age.
My father's age is three times my age
and my sister is three years younger than I am.
If I am n years old and the combined age of all four of us is 157, how old am I?

16 years old

My age: n   *Grandfather: $5n$*   *Father: $3n$*   *Sister: $n-3$*
Equation: $10n - 3 = 157$ $10n = 160$ $n = 16$

What is Alfred Nobel most famous for inventing?

Ⓒ Dynamite

ANSWERS

ANSWERS

Challenge 41

If a laser was bounced off a mirror on the moon,
how long would it take for the round trip to the moon and back?

Ⓑ 2.5 seconds

What does FDIC stand for?

Federal Deposit Insurance Corporation

All planets rotate in the same direction except one.
Which planet is it?

Venus

In 2008, hydroelectricity supplied approximately
___ percent of the world's electricity.

Ⓓ 15% - 20%

What happened to Czar Romanov and his family
after the Bolshevik Revolution in 1917?

Ⓓ They were imprisoned and then they were executed

Lynn's wage is n dollars per hour plus a bonus of $25 per week.
What is Lynn's yearly salary when she works a 40-hour week?

52(40n + 25)   **2080n + 1300**

Weekly salary: 40n + $25   *Yearly: 52(40n + 25)*

Modern wind turbines usually have
3 blades which can reach speeds (at the tip) of :

Ⓓ 200 mph

ANSWERS

ANSWERS

Challenge 42

How far will a car travel in 45 seconds if its speed is 60 miles per hour?

.75 miles

Distance = Speed x Time   Time is given in hours.
Because there are 45 seconds in an hour, 45 seconds is 45/3600 or .0125 hours.
$n = 60 \times .0125$ $n = .75$ miles

Alternate method: You will travel one mile in one minute at a speed of 60 miles per hour. In 45 seconds (or 3/4 of a minute) you will travel 3/4 of a mile.

Until 1971, the United States regulated the value of gold. The price of gold was set at _____.

Ⓐ **$35 per ounce**

Humans have 46 chromosomes.
One type of ant has the fewest number of chromosomes. How many?

Ⓐ **2 chromosomes**

The ant (Myrmecia croslandi) has the least number of any known organism with only a single pair of chromosomes. (Males have only a single chromosome.)

The Panama Canal was one of the most difficult engineering projects ever attempted. How many people lost their lives during the building of the Panama Canal? (French and American)

Ⓒ **25,000**

It is estimated that over 25,000 workers lost their lives during the long and dangerous project. (Most dying from disease and landslides)

The majority of the Vikings came from three countries. Name two.

Denmark, Norway and Sweden

The charge to rent a car is $19.95 per day plus $.12 per mile. What is the cost of renting a car for n days when it is driven t miles?

$19.95n + .12t$

In 1997 wind power generated only 0.1% of the world's electricity. What percent of the world's electricity was generated by wind power in 2010?

Ⓒ **2.5%**

ANSWERS

ANSWERS
Challenge 43

A coin is flipped three times. If any of the three flips are heads, you win the game. What is your probability of winning?

7/8

The only way you can lose is if tails is flipped three times in a row.

The probability of flipping three tails in a row: $\frac{1}{2} \times \frac{1}{2} \times \frac{1}{2} = \frac{1}{8}$

If the probability of losing is 1/8, then the probability of winning is 7/8.

How many 2011 United State's dollars would you need to have the same buying power of one United State's dollar in 1960?

Ⓒ **$7.46**

Water boils at 212°F. At what temperature does liquid nitrogen boil?

Ⓓ **-321°F**

The Delaware Aqueduct is drilled through solid rock and is the longest tunnel in the world (as of 2010). How long is it?

Ⓑ **85 miles**

Who said the following quote?

"Mr. Gorbachev, tear down this wall."

Ronald Reagan at the Berlin Wall in 1987

A cell phone company charges $40 per month plus $.08 per text. What is the monthly bill for someone who makes *n* texts each month?

$40 + $.08n

Jeanne Calment is thought to be the person to have lived the longest. She was _____ when she died in 1997.

Ⓑ **122 years old**

ANSWERS

ANSWERS

Challenge 44

 The weight of a million dollars worth of pennies (a little over 3.1 grams each) is equivalent to the weight of how many mini-vans?

Ⓓ 170 mini-vans

 A 2011 dollar has the same buying power as how much money in 1960?

Ⓐ 13 cents

 In what year did a person first see a live cell through a microscope?

Ⓑ 1674

 What percent of volcanic activity takes place in the oceans?

Ⓓ 80%

Which U.S. president said the following quote?

"A house divided against itself cannot stand."

Abraham Lincoln

on the importance of national reconciliation during his speech at the Illinois' State Republican Convention in 1858

Ian had 4 more dimes than quarters. He also has 4 fewer nickels than quarters. What is the value of his coins if he has n quarters?

$40n + 20$

Quarters: n Dimes: $n+4$ Nickels $n-4$ Value of quarters: $25n$
Value of dimes: $10(n+4)$ $10n + 40$
Value of nickels $5(n-4)$ $5n - 20$
Total value: $25n + 10n + 40 + 5n - 20$
$40n + 20$

 Airbags in cars sometimes deploy without the car being involved in an accident. What triggers the deployment?

Ⓐ The car hits a pothole

ANSWERS

ANSWERS

Challenge 45

What is 1% of 1% of $100?

One cent

A 2011 dollar has the same buying power as how much money in 1914?

Ⓐ **5 cents**

In what year was the sound barrier officially broken in a manned aircraft?

Ⓑ **1947**

The second largest lake in the world is Lake Superior with an area of 31,820 square miles. The largest lake in the world is the Caspian Sea. It has an area that is _____ times the size of Lake Superior.

Ⓓ **4.5**

Which U.S. president said the following quote? "Ask not what your country can do for you, ask what you can do for your country."

John Kennedy

during his inauguration speech in 1960.

Amy always saves 1/4 of her allowance. If Amy's allowance is *n* dollars per week, what will she have saved in a year?

13*n*

Amy's allowance for a year is 52*n*. 1/4 of 52*n* = 13*n*

How many gallons of air does the average person breathe each day?

Ⓒ **3000 gallons**

ANSWERS

ANSWERS

Challenge 46

If a bank pays 3% annual interest, the interest for one day if you deposit $1000 is 8 cents. What is the interest earned for one day if you have one billion dollars in the bank?

Ⓒ **$82,200**

If instead of buying a $6000 laptop from Apple in 1997, you bought Apple stock, your $6000 investment would be worth _____ today.

Ⓒ **$350,000**

What is the reason that a loud noise is heard during the crack of a whip?

The sound barrier is broken and a sonic boom is created.

What percent of the earth's water is saltwater?

Ⓓ **97%**

Which president of the United States said the following quote?

"I am not a crook."

Richard Nixon discussing the Watergate scandal in 1973

If a kangaroo can hop at a speed of *n* miles per hour, what is its speed in miles per minute?

n/60

There are 60 minutes in an hour, so it would go 1/60 of the distance in a minute.

Blue whales can communicate with other whales at a distance of _____ miles.

Ⓓ **1000 miles**

ANSWERS

ANSWERS

Challenge 47

How many liters of water will fit into one cubic meter?

 1000

*There are 10 x 10 x 10 cubic decimeters in a cubic meter.
A liter of water is by definition a cubic decimeter of water.*

If an $800 profit is going to be split between three people in a ratio of 5:3:2, what does the person receive who will receive the least amount?

$160

*In a 5:3:2 ratio, there are 5+3+2 = 10 parts
$800 ÷ 10 = $80 per part
2 x $80 = $160*

At what speed, in miles per hour, does a plane break the sound barrier?
(at sea level)

 760 mph

What percent of the earth's freshwater is frozen?

 **65%**

Which president of the United States said the following quote?
"In the councils of government, we must guard against the acquisition of unwarranted influence, whether sought or unsought, by the military-industrial complex. The potential for the disastrous rise of misplaced power exists and will persist."

Dwight Eisenhower in his farewell address in 1961

If a kangaroo can hop at a speed of *n* miles per hour, what is its speed in miles per second?

***n*/3600**

*There are 3600 seconds in an hour, so it would go
1/3600 of the distance in a second.*

What percent of an iceberg is below the surface of the water?

Ⓒ **90%**

ANSWERS

ANSWERS

Challenge 48

What is the surface area of a cubic yard expressed in square feet?

54 square feet

Each face of a cubic yard is 3 x 3 = 9 square feet
6 faces x 9 = 54 square feet

$30,000 has been charged on a credit card with an annual interest rate of 20%. If only the interest is paid each month, what is the monthly payment?

Ⓒ **$500**

.20 x $30,000 = $6000 interest in a year $6000 ÷ 12 = $500 per month

Galapagos tortoises have one of the longest life spans of animals. Mayflies have one of the shortest life spans of _____ days.

Ⓑ **.5**

Name four of the five most populated states.
1. **California - 36,457,549**
2. **Texas - 23,507,783**
3. **New York - 19,306,183**
4. **Florida - 18,089,888**
5. **Illinois - 12,831,970**

Which president of the United States said the following quote?

"The only thing we have to fear is fear itself."

Franklin Roosevelt in his inaugural address in 1933

If a kangaroo can hop at a speed of n miles per hour, what is its speed in feet per hour?

$5280n$

There are 5280 feet in one mile, so the kangaroo will travel 5280 times the number of miles.

A cockroach can live _____ without a head.

Ⓓ **weeks**

ANSWERS

ANSWERS

Challenge 49

What is the measure of angle b?

Ⓒ 180° minus angle a

What was the minimum wage in 1970?

Ⓑ $1.60 per hour

There are 206 bones in the human body.
What percent of the 206 bones are hand and foot bones?

Ⓒ 50%

Name three of the five least populated states.

46. South Dakota - 781,919   47. Alaska - 670,053
48. North Dakota - 635,867   49. Vermont - 623,908
50. Wyoming - 515,004

Which president of the United States said the following two quotes?

"A statesman is a politician who's been dead 10 or 15 years."

"It's a recession when your neighbor loses his job;
it's a depression wen you lose yours."

Harry S. Truman   April of 1958

If a kangaroo can hop at a speed of n miles per hour,
what is its speed in feet per minute?

$$\frac{5280n}{60}$$

If the kangaroo travels 5280n feet per hour,
it travels 1/60 of the distance in a minute.

What is the approximate weight of a paper clip?

Ⓒ 1 gram

ANSWERS

ANSWERS

Challenge 50

What is the speed of a car if it travels one mile in 40 seconds?

90 miles per hour

Distance = Speed x Time (in hours)

1 mile = n x 40/3600   1 = n x .0111   1 = .0111n   n = 90 mph

If you work a 40-hour week for 52 weeks at the current minimum wage of $7.25, what do you earn in a year?

Ⓑ **$15,000**

40 hours x 52 weeks = 2080 hours   2080 x $7.25 = $15,080

What is another name for the breastbone?

Sternum

Canada has ten provinces and three territories. Name six.

Northwest Territories	**Nunavut**	**Manitoba**	**Yukon**
British Columbia	**Quebec**	**Nova Scotia**	
New Brunswick	**Ontario**	**Saskatchewan**	
Prince Edward Island	**Alberta**	**Newfoundland**	**and Labrador**

Which president of the United States said the following quote?

"We look forward to a world founded upon four essential human freedoms. The first is freedom of speech and expression everywhere in the world. The second is freedom of every person to worship God in his own way-everywhere in the world. The third is freedom from want. ... The fourth is freedom from fear."

Franklin Roosevelt on January 6, 1941 in a message to Congress

If a kangaroo can hop at a speed of *n* miles per hour, what is its speed in feet per second?

$$\frac{5280n}{3600}$$

5280 feet in a mile and 3600 seconds in an hour

The record for the longest scientifically documented period without sleep is:

Ⓓ **264**

(The lack of sleep caused hallucinations, paranoia, blurred vision, slurred speech and memory and concentration lapses.)

ANSWERS

ANSWERS

Challenge 51

A circular sprinkler at the center of a square garden waters every part of the garden except the corners. If the garden is a square with sides of 20 feet, how many square feet of the garden does the sprinkler not water?

86 square feet

Area of garden: 20 x 20 = 400 square feet
Area of circle: 3.14 x 10 x 10 = 314 square feet
Unwatered part: 400 - 314 = 86 square feet

The median U.S. wage in 2010 was $26,363. If it is assumed that this is for a 40-hour week, what is the hourly wage when one is paid $26,363 per year?

Ⓑ **$12.65**

Hours in year: 52 x 40 = 2080 $26,363 ÷ 2080 = $12.67

Tell whether each of the following is a base or an acid:

Ⓐ **Bleach (Base)**   Ⓑ **Vinegar (Acid)**
Ⓒ **Peanut Butter (Acid)**   Ⓓ **Drain Cleaner (Base)**

If the earth's population continues to double every 40 years, how many years will it be until the weight of all people on the earth is equal to the weight/mass of the entire earth?

Ⓐ **1500 years**

The total number of voting members in the House of Representatives is set by law at_____.

Ⓑ **435**

If Lori travels at 55 mph for n hours, how far did she travel?
(Distance equals Speed x Time)

55n

On a warm day, oxygen molecules travel at an average speed of:

Ⓓ **1000 mph**

ANSWERS

ANSWERS

Challenge 52

In the sequence 1,4,9,16,25, the 6th number is 36. What is the 100th number?

Ⓒ **10,000**

A day after a snow storm, 1/2 the snow melted. The next day, 1/4 of the remaining snow melted. What fraction of the snow from the storm is now left?

3/8

1/4 of the remaining 1/2 melted   1/4 of 1/2 = 1/8 melted, so 3/8 is left

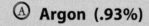

Air is made up of many elements and compounds. The top three are nitrogen, oxygen and _____.

Ⓐ **Argon (.93%)**

Carbon dioxide (.04%)   Neon (.002%)   Helium (.0005%)

How long is the "Chunnel" between England and France?

Ⓓ **31.4 miles**

Each representative in the House of Representatives serves for a _____ term.

Ⓐ **two-year**

Sara travels at 55 mph for n hours. Daniel travels five more hours than Sara, but at a speed of 30 mph. How far did they each travel?

Sara's distance: $55n$

Daniel's distance: $30n + 150$

Distance = Speed x Time   Sara's distance: $55n$
Daniel's distance: $30(n+5)$ or $30n + 150$

Category 5 hurricanes have wind speeds over:

Ⓒ **155 mph**

ANSWERS

ANSWERS

Challenge 53

How many miles does light travel in a year?

5,865,696,000,000 miles

186,000 miles per second x 86,400 seconds in a day x 365 days in a year = 5,865,696,000,000 miles

The weight of a million one dollar bills is equivalent to the weight of how many medium sized cars?

Ⓓ **Less than one**

How many skin cells do humans lose each minute?

Ⓑ **40,000**

What percent of the world's population died during the flu pandemic of 1918?

Ⓐ **2-3%**

Each U.S. state is represented by two senators, regardless of population. Senators serve _____ terms.

Ⓒ **six-year**

Sara travels at 55 mph for *n* hours. Daniel travels five more hours than Sara, but at a speed of 30 mph. How many hours until Daniel catches up with Sara?

In 11 hours

Sara's distance: 55n   Daniel's distance: 30n + 150
Set the distances equal to each other: 55n = 30n + 150   25n = 150   n = 6

F5 tornadoes have winds over:

Ⓑ **260 mph**

ANSWERS

ANSWERS
Challenge 54

A light year is the distance light travels in a year.
How far is a "sound year" in miles? *(Sound travels .2 miles per second.)*

6,307,200 miles

Sounds travels .2 miles each second x 31,536,000 seconds in a year = 6,307,200

For the next 64 days, pennies are placed on the squares of a chess board. 1st square - 1 penny • 2nd square - 2 pennies 3rd square - 4 pennies • 4th square - 8 pennies • 5th square - 16 pennies
The number of pennies will double each day. What is the height of the stack of pennies placed on the 64th square? (A penny is 1/16 inch thick.)

Ⓓ **It will be almost halfway to the star Alpha Centauri A**

1/16 inch x 2^{63} = approximately 1.5 light years

What is the largest living thing on earth?

Ⓑ **A fungus in Oregon**

World War I claimed an estimated 16 million lives.
How many lives were lost during the flu pandemic of 1918?

Ⓑ **50,000,000**

The United State's Senate has several exclusive powers. Which of the following powers does the United State's Senate not have?

Ⓐ **Power to impeach the president**

If Distance = Speed x Time, what does Time equal?

Distance

Speed

What is the weight of a British stone in pounds?

14 pounds

ANSWERS

ANSWERS

Challenge 55

How many cups are in a gallon?

Ⓐ **16**

If $100 loses 10% of its value each year, how many years until the original $100 is worth less than $50?

7 years

Multiply by 90% or .9 each year:
1st year: $90   2nd: $81   3rd: $72.90   4th: $65.61
5th: $59.05   6th: $53.14   7th: $47.83

The weight of a blue whale's heart is approximately 3000 times the weight of a human's heart. The weight of a blue whale's brain is _____ times the weight of a human's brain.

Ⓐ **5 times**

Greenland is considered the world's largest island. What is the second largest island?

New Guinea

The Constitution requires that the president be at least _____ years old.

Ⓑ **35**

Rachel starts a bike trip at the beginning of a bike trail and travels at 10 mph. Jon starts his bike trip two hours later at the same spot and travels at 15 mph. How long until Jon catches up with Rachel? (Remember that Distance = Speed x Time)

4 hours from when Jon started

Rachel's speed: 10 mph   Rachel's time: n
Jon's speed: 15 mph   Jon's time: n - 2 (He started 2 hours later)
Rachel's distance: 10 mph x n   Jon's distance: 15 mph x n-2
They will meet when the distances are equal: 10n = 15(n-2)   10n = 15n - 30
5n = 30   n = 6

How many breaths does a typical person take in a lifetime?

Ⓒ **600,000,000**

ANSWERS

ANSWERS

Challenge 56

If sound and light had a race across a football field of 100 yards starting from one goal line to the other, how far would sound have traveled when light travels the 100 yards to win the race?

© .004 inches

There are 1760 yards in a mile, so light travels 1760 x 186,000 = 327,360,000 yards in a second.

$$\frac{327,360,000 \text{ (yards)}}{1 \text{ second}} = \frac{100 \text{ (yards)}}{n \text{ (seconds)}}$$

$$327,360,000n = 100$$

n = 1/3,273,600 = .000,000,3 seconds for light to travel 100 yards
Sound travels 1100 feet per second or
13,200 inches per second x .000,000,3 seconds = .00396 inches

If the exchange rate is one dollar equals .80 euros, how many dollars would you receive for one euro?

$$\frac{\$1}{.80 \text{ euros}} = \frac{n \text{ (dollars)}}{1 \text{ (euro)}} \quad \textbf{\$1.25}$$

.80n = 1   n = 1/.8 or $1.25

The ratio of brain weight to body weight in a human is 1/40. What is the ratio of brain weight to body weight in a lion?

Ⓓ 1/550 (A lion brain is approximately 1/2 pound.)

What percent of Europe's population died from the Black Plague in the outbreak that occurred in the 1300's?

© 30% - 60%

The amendments that most people are familiar with are the first and second amendments. What are they?

1. Freedom of Speech, Press, Religion and Petition
2. Right to keep and bear arms

If $E = mc^2$, then what does m equal?

$$m = \frac{E}{c^2}$$

The gas mileage for a Toyota Prius is 51 miles per gallon. What is the mileage for a M1 Abrams Main Battle Tank?

Ⓐ .6 mpg

ANSWERS

ANSWERS

Challenge 57

The probability of at least two people having matching birthdays in a group of 23 people is:

Ⓐ **1 in 2**

When mortgage interest rates were 3%, a bank told a family that it could afford a home up to a cost of $300,000. If mortgage interest rates climb to 9%, what price home can the same family afford? (30 year mortgage)

Ⓑ **$150,000**

(Use mortgage calculator)

While awake, a human brain generates enough power to light a:

Ⓐ **15-watt light bulb**

The Mt. St. Helens eruption changed the lives of thousands of people and turned millions of acres of forest into a wasteland.
When did Mt. St. Helens erupt?

Ⓒ **1980**

Before the Pony Express, it took mail a month to travel from Missouri to California by stagecoach.
The Pony Express took ____ days to travel from Missouri to California.

Ⓑ **10**

Use the formula for changing Celsius into Fahrenheit to find a formula for changing Fahrenheit into Celsius. Fahrenheit = Celsius x 1.8 + 32

$$C = \frac{F - 32}{1.8}$$

$F = 1.8C + 32$
Subtract 32 from both sides: $F - 32 = 1.8C$
Divide both sides by 1.8: $C = \frac{F - 32}{1.8}$

The gas tank capacity of a Toyota Prius is 11.9 gallons.
What is the gas tank capacity of a M1 Abrams Main Battle Tank?

Ⓓ **500 gallons**

ANSWERS

ANSWERS

Challenge 58

Is n^2 ever smaller than n?

Ⓑ **Only when n is a fraction between 0 and 1**

How much did the space shuttle program cost each of the 313,000,000 people in the United States? (divided evenly)

Ⓑ **$675**

Humans have a ratio of brain weight to body weight of 1/40. Match the following animals with their ratio of brain weight to body weight:

Cat - Shark - Small bird   1/2500   1/12   1/100

Cat 1/100   Shark 1/2500   Small bird 1/12

Norilsk, Russia is the northern most city in the world. What is its average temperature?

Ⓒ **9°F**

What is the salary for members of the House of Representatives and the Senate?

Ⓒ **$174,000**

The number of cats is n; the number of dogs is $2n$ and the number of ostriches is $4n$. How many total legs are there?

$20n$

Cat legs: $4 \times n = 4n$ Dog legs: $4 \times 2n = 8n$ Ostrich legs: $2 \times 4n = 8n$

Humans use _____ of their brains.

Ⓓ **100%**

The statement, "We use only 10% of our brains" is false; it's a myth. We use all of our brain.

ANSWERS

ANSWERS

Challenge 59

What is the probability of rolling 5 of a kind when 5 dice are rolled?

Ⓒ **1/1296**

The first roll can be any number, then there is a
1 in 6 probability of each roll matching that original number.

$$\frac{1}{1} \times \frac{1}{6} \times \frac{1}{6} \times \frac{1}{6} \times \frac{1}{6} = \frac{1}{1296}$$

A family in the United States spends, on average,
what percent of its income on food each year?
(Food at home and away)

Ⓐ **13%**   *$6372*

Female tarantulas live 30 years or longer.
How long do male tarantulas live?

Ⓒ **5-10 years**

If all the Arctic ice melts, how high will the sea level rise?

Ⓐ **It won't rise**

(In the Arctic, ice floats on the ocean.)

The House of Representatives has several exclusive powers. Which of the following powers does the House of Representatives not have?

Ⓒ **Power to put the president on trial**

A cube has sides that are *n* inches long.
What is the volume of the cube?

n^3

n x *n* x *n* = n^3

The normal temperature for the human body is 98.6°F.
The highest human body temperature ever recorded was:

Ⓓ **115.7° F**

(The cause was heatstroke --- he did survive)

ANSWERS

ANSWERS

Challenge 60

If a die is rolled three separate times, what is the probability that you will not roll any "4"s?

Ⓓ 125/216

Each time you roll, the probability that you will not roll a "4" is 5/6.

$$\frac{5}{6} \times \frac{5}{6} \times \frac{5}{6} = \frac{125}{216}$$

Before the Civil War, the average Southern family spent 6-7 dollars a month on food. By 1864, this increased to _____ per month.

Ⓑ $90-$100

Name Newton's first law of motion.

An object in motion tends to stay in motion unless an external force is applied to it.

Where is the driest place on earth?

Ⓓ Antarctica

The Dry Valley's region of Antarctica has had no precipitation in 2 million years.

Which amendment allows a citizen to refuse to testify against him or herself?

Fifth amendment

A person with $1,000,000 gives $100 to a charity. How much should a person with n dollars donate to charity to give the same proportional amount?

.0001n

$$\frac{\$100}{\$1,000,000} = .0001$$

Person gave .0001 of money. A person with n money should give .0001n

How far apart are railroad tracks?

Ⓐ 4 feet 8.5 inches

ANSWERS

ANSWERS

Challenge 61

How many cubic inches are in a cubic yard?

46,656 cubic inches

36 x 36 x 36 = 46,656 cubic inches

What is 1/4% of $100?

25 cents

A human has a heart that is approximately 1% the size of a human body. The size of a blue whale heart is what percent of the entire whale?

Ⓐ **1%**

When did Hawaii become a state?

Ⓒ **1959**

Each state receives representation in the House of Representatives in proportion to its population, but is entitled to at least one representative. The most populous state, California, currently has 53 representatives. How many states only have one representative in the House of Representatives?

Ⓓ **7**

Juan's expenses for a dinner are $12 for a taxi, *n* dollars for a meal plus a 15% tip for the waitress. What is the total cost of the dinner plus taxi?

1.15*n* + $12

Meal: n   Tip: .15n   Taxi: $12

Red blood cells were discovered by Jan Swammerdam in___.

Ⓐ **1658**

ANSWERS

ANSWERS

Challenge 62

What is 1/2 of 1/2 of 1/2 of 1/2?

1/16

An ad for a "gold" coin says that for $19.95 you can get a genuine gold clad coin that contains a full 14 milligrams of gold. If gold cost $1500 per ounce, what is the value of 14 milligrams of gold?

Ⓐ **75 cents**

The heaviest documented primate on record belongs to what species?

Human   (A morbidly obese human)

Alaska was purchased for _____ dollars in 1867.

Ⓒ **7.2 million**

Each state receives representation in the House of Representatives in proportion to its population, but is entitled to at least one representative. The most populous state, California, currently has 53 representatives. There are currently seven states with only one representative. Name five.

Alaska, Delaware, South Dakota, North Dakota, Vermont, Wyoming, Montana

There are a total of 19 grasshoppers and tarantulas. If the number of grasshoppers is called n, how many tarantula eyes are there? How many tarantula legs?

Eyes: $8(19-n)$ Legs: $8(19-n)$

There are $19-n$ tarantulas. They each have eight eyes and also eight legs.

The mammal with the fastest heartbeat is the pygmy shrew. The mammal with the slowest heartbeat is the blue whale. What is the ratio of the heartbeat of a pygmy shrew to the heartbeat of a blue whale?

pygmy / blue whale =

Ⓒ **150/1**

pygmy shrew: 1200   blue whale: 8   1200/8 = 150

ANSWERS

ANSWERS

Challenge 63

A cubic decimeter of water weighs one kilogram.
What is the weight of a cubic meter of water?

1000 kilograms

There are 10 x 10 x 10 = 1000 cubic decimeters in a cubic meter.

Put in order from smallest to largest:

.07 cents $.06   8 cents

Change to all cents: $.06= 6 cents   .07 cent =7/100 of a cent
8 cents = 8 cents

The earth rotates at a speed of 1000 miles per hour.
How fast does the moon rotate?

Ⓐ **10 mph**

Alaska was purchased from Russia in 1867.
What was the price per acre?

Ⓑ **2 cents**

The amendments listed below are all included in the Bill of Rights.

Name the number for each amendment.
Right to a speedy trial, witnesses, etc. **Sixth Amendment**
Right to a trial by jury **Seventh Amendment**
Outlaws excessive bail and cruel punishment **Eighth Amendment**

The price of a book after a 15% discount is 8.5n.
What was the original price of the book?

10n

After a 15% discount the book cost 8.5n means: .85 x something = 8.5n
Divide both sides by .85   something = 10n

How many new cells does the human body make each day?

Ⓓ **24 billion**

ANSWERS

ANSWERS

Challenge 64

You are facing a cliff that is an unknown distance away. If you shout towards the cliff, it takes 15 seconds for the echo to reach your ears. How far away is the cliff?

Ⓐ **1.5 miles**

It takes sound 5 seconds to travel one mile, so the sound traveled 3 miles. Because the 3 miles was a round trip to the cliff and back, the cliff must be half of 3 miles.

If apples are .60 cents each, what is the cost of 5 apples?

Ⓐ **3 cents**

.60 cents is 6/10 of a cent. 5 x 6/10 = 3 cents

How many cells are in a typical human body?

Ⓓ **50 - 100 trillion**

Name the state where each mountain is located.
- Mt. McKinley: **Alaska**
- Pikes Peak: **Colorado**
- Mt. Ranier: **Washington**

Put the following inventions in order from earliest invented to most recent:
- **Lighter: 16th century**
- **Hot air balloon: 1783**
- **Matches: 1805**
- **Telephone: 1876**

A painting and a frame together cost $800. If the painting cost $700 more than the frame, what is the cost of the frame?

$50

Frame: n   Painting: n + $700   Add: 2n + $700 = $800   n = $50

Gold is so malleable that a small amount can be stretched very far. How long a wire can be made from one ounce of gold?

Ⓓ **62 miles**

ANSWERS

ANSWERS

Challenge 65

A microsecond is a millionth of a second and a picosecond is a trillionth of a second. What part of a microsecond is a picosecond?

1/1,000,000 or one millionth

Two cars each travel 15,000 miles each year. One gets 50 miles per gallon of gas while the other gets 40 miles per gallon. If gas cost $4.00 per gallon, how much less money does gas cost in the 50 mpg car? (for one year)

$300

50 mpg car uses 15,000 ÷ 50 = 300 gallons of gas x $4 = $1200
40 mpg car uses 15,000 ÷ 40 = 375 gallons of gas x $4 = $1500

How many watts are in a kilowatt?

1000

Name the state where each mountain is located.
- **Mt. Hood:** **Oregon**
- **Mt. Washington:** **New Hampshire**
- **Mt. St. Helens:** **Washington**

An estimated _____ Americans died during the flu pandemic of 1918-1919.

ⓒ **675,000**

A hill was climbed at a speed of *n* miles per hour. The descent was at a speed of 3*n* mph. What was the average speed for the entire trip?

1.5*n*

Count n three times for the trip up the hill because it took three times as long as the descent. n + n + n + 3n = 6n
6n ÷ 4 = 1.5n   (Divide by four because four "things" were added.)

The earth gets heavier every day because of falling space dust. How much heavier does the earth get each day?

Ⓑ **100 tons**

ANSWERS

ANSWERS

Challenge 66

If 28 people each ate 3/4 of a pie,
how many pies did they eat?

21 pies

28 x 3/4 = 84/4 = 21

An apple and a pear together cost 90 cents.
If the apple cost twice as much as the pear, what did the apple cost?

60 cents

What is the life span of a red blood cell?

Ⓑ **120 days**

Some states have capitals that are not their largest city,
and because of this, many people answer incorrectly when asked
for those states' capitals. What are the capitals of the following states:
(Answer three out of the four correctly)

Alaska:	**Juneau**
California:	**Sacramento**
Illinois:	**Springfield**
Michigan:	**Lansing**

Polio epidemics increased in size and frequency in the late 1940's and
early 1950's before the introduction of the polio vaccine. On average,
how many cases of polio occurred each year in the United States
in the 1940's and early 50's before the polio vaccine?

Ⓑ **35,000**

There are five consecutive even numbers.
If the first is n, what are the other four?

$n+2 \quad n+4 \quad n+6 \quad n+8$

17,228 players have played baseball in the major leagues.
What percent made it to the Hall of Fame?

Ⓑ **1.35%**

ANSWERS

ANSWERS

Challenge 67

What is 1/10 divided by 1/100?

10

The question really asks how many 1/100 will fit into 1/10. Answer: 10

A store is having a sale with discounts as shown below. If the regular price starts at $100 on Sunday, what will the price be on Friday?

$1

Sunday: Regular price
Monday: 80% off: Discount is .8 x $100 = $80 New price: $20
Tuesday: Additional 75% off Monday's price is $5
Wednesday: Additional 20% off Tuesday's price is $4
Thursday: Additional 50% off Wednesday's price is $2
Friday: Additional 50% off Thursday's price is $1

What is the life span of a white blood cell?

Ⓐ **14 days**

Some states have capitals that are not their largest city, and because of this, many people answer incorrectly when asked for those states' capitals. What are the capitals of the following states:
(Answer three out of the four correctly)

Nevada: Carson City   **Pennsylvania: Harrisburg**

Texas: Austin   **Washington: Olympia**

All of the following have had polio except one. Name him or her.

Dustin Hoffman did not have polio

There are five consecutive odd numbers. If the first is *n*, what are the other four?

$n + 2$ $n + 4$ $n + 6$ $n + 8$

The average barometric pressure at sea level is 29.92 inches of mercury. What is the lowest barometric pressure ever recorded on earth?

Ⓑ **25.69 inches of mercury**

The lowest pressure ever measured was 25.69 inches during Typhoon Tip in the western Pacific Ocean. It occurred on Oct. 12, 1979.

ANSWERS

ANSWERS

Challenge 68

One definition of a meter is:
"The distance light travels in 1/299,792,458 of a second."
How many meters will light travel in one second?

299,792,458 meters in one second

What fraction of Americans own their home?

 2/3

What is the life span of a liver cell?

Ⓒ **18 months**

How many square miles was the largest iceberg on record?
(Square miles above the water level)

Ⓓ **4,200 square miles.**

183 miles long and 23 miles wide

During the period known as The Dark Ages, Rome and other cities deteriorated because of the invasions of barbarians from northern and central Europe. The term Dark Ages refers to the five hundred years following the fall of Rome. What time period was it?

Ⓑ **500 AD - 1000 AD**

On September 15, 2010, Luke is twice as old as Rachel who is twice as old as Daniel. If Daniel is n, then what will Luke's age be on September 15, 2013?

$4n + 3$

Luke's age 2010: $4n$
Luke's age 2013: $4n + 3$

The average barometric pressure at sea level is 29.92 inches of mercury. What is the highest barometric pressure ever recorded on earth?

Ⓐ **32.01**

ANSWERS

ANSWERS

Challenge 69

If the radius of a circle is cut in half,
the area of the new circle is what fraction of the original circle?

1/4

Circle with a 4 inch radius has an area of 16π
Circle with a 2 inch radius has an area of 4π

A credit card is used to charge a $500 computer. If the annual interest rate is 34.9% and only the minimum monthly payment of $15 is paid, how long will it take to pay off the credit card debt?

Ⓒ **10 years**   *(Use mortgage calculator)*

What is the life span of a nerve cell?

Ⓓ **100 years**

What is the combined population of Canada and Mexico?

Ⓐ **147 million**

(Canada: 33 million   Mexico: 114 million)

In what year did the Battle of the Alamo take place?

Ⓑ **1836**

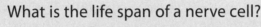

A blue whale is 5 times the weight of a brontosaurus, which is 7 times the weight of a tyrannosaurus rex. If the combined weight of all three is 215 tons, what does the tyrannosaurus rex weigh?

5 tons

tyrannosaurus rex: n brontosaurus: $7n$
blue whale: $35n$ $43n = 215$ $n = 5$

As the altitude increases, the oxygen content of the air decreases dramatically. At the top of Mount Everest, there is what fraction of the oxygen in the air as compared to sea level?

Ⓒ **1/3**

ANSWERS

ANSWERS

Challenge 70

If a ruler has a shadow of 4 inches,
how long a shadow would a yardstick have?

One Foot

A credit card is used to charge a $500 computer.
If the annual interest rate is 29.9% and only the minimum monthly
payment of $13.14 is paid, the debt will be paid off in 10 years.
How much total interest will be paid for the $500 loan?

Ⓒ **$1077.28**   (Use mortgage calculator)

Trees receive an estimated _____ percent of their nutrition from the
atmosphere and _____ percent from the soil.

Ⓐ **90% -- 10%**

The United States has 50 states while Canada has
10 provinces and 3 territories. How is Mexico divided?

Ⓑ **It has 31 states**

What year did the Battle of the Little Bighorn
(Custer's Last Stand) take place?

Ⓒ **1876**

Car rental company A charges $40 per day plus 8 cents per mile.
Car rental company B charges $120 per day, but does not charge for
miles driven. How many miles must one drive to have
the charges from both companies be the same?

1000 miles per day

Company A charge per day: $40 + $.08m
Company B charge per day: $120
Set charges equal to each other:
$120 = $40 + $.08m   .08m = $80   m = 1000

The record height for a parachute jump is:

Ⓓ **19.5 miles**   (From a balloon)

ANSWERS

ANSWERS

Challenge 71

If you walked up a hill at a speed of 3 miles per hour and then down the same path at a speed of 6 miles per hour, what would be your average speed for your walk?

Ⓐ 4 mph

You need to count the 3 mph twice because you spent twice as long walking 3 mph compared to 6 mph. 3 + 3 + 6 = 12
12 ÷ 3 = 4 mph

A $25,000 car cost $27,250 when sales tax is added. What is the sales tax rate?

9%

Sales tax of $2,250 is what percent of $25,000. $2,250 ÷ $25,000 = .09 or 9%

How much would a person who weighs 200 pounds on earth weigh on a neutron star?

Ⓓ 28,000,000,000,000 pounds

Put these places in order from north to south:
Northern tip of Maine -- London -- Halifax, Nova Scotia.

Ⓑ London; Northern tip of Maine; Halifax, Nova Scotia

Terrible conditions for children who worked in factories in England in the 1830's led to laws that protected child workers. One 1830's law said that no one under the age of _____ could work in factories.

Ⓑ 9 years old

If a 10' by 50' wall can be painted in 5 hours, how much of the wall can be painted in *n* hours?

n/5

One hour: 1/5   2 hours: 2/5   3 hours 3/5   *n* hours n/5

What planet has the longest day and which one has the shortest day?

Venus has the longest day --- 243 Earth days
Jupiter has the shortest day --- 10 hours

ANSWERS

ANSWERS

Challenge 72

50% of the students at Glenwood University are women; 25% of the women play chess; 10% of the women who play chess are experts; 50% of the women experts are left-handed. If 10 of the women chess experts are left-handed, how many students attend Glenwood University?

Ⓑ **1600**

What is the cost of smoking two packs of cigarettes a day for a year if you live in New York City and buy your cigarettes there?

Ⓓ **$10,950**

How much would a person who weighs 200 pounds on earth weigh on our sun?

Ⓒ **5500 pounds**

The Richter Scale is a way to quantify the energy contained in an earthquake. The difference in ground motion between a magnitude 6 earthquake and a magnitude 8 earthquake is how many times stronger in a magnitude 8 earthquake?

The magnitude 8 is 100 times stronger than the magnitude 6

A child labor law passed in the 1840's in England said that children under the age of 13 could work no more than _____ hours per week.

Ⓒ **36**

A television that normally sells for *n* dollars is on sale for 25% off. What is the total price for the television if the sales tax rate is 6%?

.795n

New price: .75n x 1.06 = .795n

What is the height of the world's tallest building? (Dubai)

Ⓑ **2723 feet**

ANSWERS

ANSWERS
Challenge 73

How many cubic yards of cement will be used in a driveway that is 3 yards wide, 9 yards long and one foot thick?

9 cubic yards

3 yards x 9 yards x 1/3 of a yard = 9 cubic yards

The bill for groceries was $18.37.
The clerk was given a $20 bill and 2 quarters.
What is the change?

$2.13

The Amazon rain forest produces what percent of the world's oxygen?

Ⓐ **20%**

The number of children per woman is highest in what country?

Ⓒ **Niger**

What year was the D-Day Invasion at Normandy?

Ⓒ **1944**

If Keith types 80 words per minute and there are 160 words on a page, how many minutes would it take Keith to type *n* pages?

2*n* minutes

2 minutes per page x n pages = 2n minutes

How many atoms are in the entire universe?

Ⓐ 10^{87}

ANSWERS

ANSWERS

Challenge 74

If a building is 20 feet tall and the base of a ladder is 15 feet from the building, how long is the ladder?

Ⓐ **25 feet**

This is a 3-4-5 triangle.   15-20-?   Answer: 25

$a^2 + b^2 = c^2$ $(15 \times 15) + (20 \times 20) = (c \times c)$

$625 = (c \times c)$ $c = 25$

A person with $1,000,000 gives $100 to a charity. How much should a person with $1000 donate to charity to give the same proportional amount?

10 cents

$\dfrac{\$100}{\$1,000,000} = \dfrac{n}{\$1000}$ $1,000,000n = 100,000$ $n = .1$ dollar or 10 cents

The unit of measure for weight in the United States is the pound. What unit is used for mass?

Ⓓ **Slug**

One of the longest bridges in the world is the Danyang-Kunshan Grand Bridge in China. How long is it?

Ⓓ **102.4 miles**

Four US presidents have been assassinated while in office. Name three.

Abraham Lincoln (1865)   **James A. Garfield (1881)**
William McKinley (1901)   **John F. Kennedy (1963)**

If Keith types 80 words per minute and there are 160 words on a page, how many hours would it take Keith to type *n* pages?

n/30

2n minutes for n pages
60 minutes in an hour so divide 2n by 60 = n/30

How long would it take for a penny dropped from the Empire State Building to hit the ground?

Ⓒ **9 seconds**

ANSWERS

ANSWERS

Challenge 75

10^{10} is how many times larger than 10^9?

Ⓓ **10 times**

10,000,000,000 ÷ 1,000,000,000 = 10

If an American went to Germany and saw that lunch was 8 euros, how many dollars would the lunch cost?
Exchange rate: 1 Euro = 1.2771 U.S. dollars

$10.22

1.2771 dollars x 8 euros = $10.2168

The unit of measure for weight in the United States is the pound. What is the unit of weight in the metric system?

Ⓐ **Newton**

(Grams and kilograms are units of mass.)

What is the largest city in China?

Ⓒ **Shanghai**

Who were the leaders of the three Allied countries during World War II?
(U.S., England and Russia)

Churchill, Roosevelt, Stalin

The formula for finding the temperature (Celsius) based on the number of cricket chirps per minute is:

Celsius = $\frac{\text{chirps per minute} + 30}{7}$

What is the formula for predicting the number of cricket chirps if you know the temperature? Chirps per minute = ?

Chirps per minute = 7c - 30

Celsius = $\frac{\text{chirps per minute} + 30}{7}$ multiply both sides by 7

7c = Chirps per minute + 30

Subtract 30 from both sides: Chirps per minute = 7c - 30

How tall is the Empire State Building with its antenna spire included?

Ⓐ **1454 feet**

ANSWERS

ANSWERS

Challenge 76

It is almost impossible to fold a paper more than 7 or 8 times, but if it were possible, how thick would a 1/32 of an inch piece of paper be if you folded it 50 times? (It will be 2/32 of an inch after it is folded once; 4/32 of an inch after it is folded twice; 8/32 after three folds; etc.)

Ⓓ **More than 50 feet**

It would end up being 555,308,902 miles tall.
1/32 inch x 2^{50} = Approximately 555,308,902 miles!!

If a German came to New York City and saw that a Broadway show cost $110, how many euros would she expect to pay?
Exchange rate: 1 Euro = 1.2771 U.S. dollars

86.13 euros

$\frac{1\ euro}{\$1.2771} = \frac{n\ euros}{\$110}$ $1.2771n = 110$ $n = 86.13\ euros$

Put the following animals in order from slowest heartbeat to fastest.
Blue whale (8), hibernating bear (14), elephant (30), human (72)

Where is the world's deepest lake?

Ⓐ **Lake Baikal - Russia**

In what year did Adolf Hitler come to power?

Ⓒ **1933**

If a heart beats 72 times per minute, how many times does it beat in *n* seconds?

1.2*n* times

The heart will beat 72/60 = 1.2 times per second
In n seconds, it will beat 1.2 x n times

Subtract the average height of a female in the United States from the average height of a male in the United States: _____ inches

Ⓒ **5.4 inches**   (69.2 inches - 63.8 inches)

ANSWERS

ANSWERS

Challenge 77

Is 5n ever larger than 10n?

ⓓ **Yes**   (negative numbers)

A Japanese visitor to Paris sees that hotel rooms cost 212 euros per night.
How many yen would he need to pay? (round to the nearest yen)
Exchange rate: 1 Euro = 1.2771 U.S. dollars
1 U.S. dollar = 76.7833 yen

20,789 yen

Exchange rate: 1 Euro = 1.2771 U.S. dollars
1 U.S. dollar = 76.7833 yen

212 euros = 212 x 1.2771 dollars = $270.75
$270.75 x 76.7833 yen per dollar = 20,789 yen

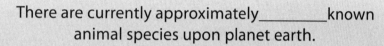

There are currently approximately _____ known
animal species upon planet earth.

ⓑ **5 - 10 million**

How deep is the world's deepest lake?

ⓒ **5369 feet**

World War I went from 1914 to 1918.
In what year did the United States enter the war?

ⓓ **1917**

If the value of a pile of coins is 82n cents,
what is the value of the coins expressed as dollars?

$.82n

To change cents to dollars, divide by 100.

The world's longest snake was a reticulated python, which was
found in Indonesia in 1912. How long was it?

ⓑ **32.75 feet**

ANSWERS

ANSWERS

Challenge 78

$1/2 + 1/4 + 1/8 + 1/16 + 1/32 + …… =$

Ⓒ **Approaches 1**

There are 500 marbles in a box. The value of a red marble is 10 cents and the value of a blue marble is 25 cents. When 50 marbles are drawn randomly from the box, there are 40 blue and 10 red marbles. Estimate the value of the box of marbles.

$110

40 : 10 ratio of the 50 marbles means the entire box has a makeup close to 400 blue and 100 red.
400 x 25 cents + 100 x 10 cents = $110

Meteors move very fast with some entering the earth's atmosphere at speeds as high as:

Ⓒ **130,000 miles per hour**

The deepest hole ever drilled by man is the Kola Superdeep Borehole (Russia). How deep was it?

Ⓑ **7.6 miles**

India gained freedom from British rule in:

Ⓒ **1947**

In a pile of nickels, dimes and quarters, there are 10 times as many quarters as dimes and twice as many dimes as nickels. If the value of the coins is $36.75, how many quarters are there?

140 quarters

Number of quarters: $20n$ Value of quarters: $25 \times 20n = 500n$
Number of dimes: $2n$ Value of dimes: $10 \times 2n = 20n$
Number of nickels: n Value of nickels: $5n$
$5n + 20n + 500n = 3675$ cents $525n = 3675$ $n = 7$ $20n = 140$

A 1985 study conducted by the science journal 'Nature' calculated the rate of meteorites hitting humans as once every_____.

Ⓓ **180 years**

ANSWERS

ANSWERS

Challenge 79

A water pipe with an eight inch diameter is replaced with one with a four inch diameter. By how much is the flow reduced through the pipe?

Ⓒ **1/4 the water**

πr^2 : Eight inch pipe has an opening of 16π
Four inch pipe has an opening of 4π

How much more interest would be earned if $8000 is invested for a year at 9% interest instead of 3% interest?

$480

.03 x $8000 = $240   .09 x $8000 = $720

There are 8 main blood types in humans. Name six of the eight.

O Positive	40 out 100	O Negative	7 out of 100
A Positive	34 out of 100	A Negative	6 out of 100
B Positive	8 out of 100	B Negative	1 out of 100
AB Positive	3 out of 100	AB Negative	1 out 200

Which country has the lowest life expectancy? (United Nations data)

Ⓐ **Mozambique** (39.2)

*Afghanistan (43.8)   Zimbabwe (43.5)
Somalia (48.2)*

Match the person with his country:

Napoleon: France
Gandhi: India
Karl Marx: Germany
Czar Romanov: Russia

How many toes are in a group of *n* people?

10*n* toes

Humans have 46 chromosomes. A type of fern called adders-tongue (Ophioglossum reticulatum) has the highest known number of chromosomes. How many chromosomes does this plant have?

Ⓓ **Over 1000** (1200)

ANSWERS

ANSWERS

Challenge 80

If a die is rolled three separate times,
what is the probability that at least one "4" will be rolled?

Ⓐ **91/216**

Probability of not rolling a "4" on all three rolls: 5/6 x 5/6 x 5/6 = 125/216

Chance of rolling at least one "4" is $1 - \frac{125}{216} = 91/216$

If $5000 is charged on a credit card that
charges 34.9% interest, how much is the interest charge for one year?

$1745

34.9% is .349   .349 x $5000 = $1745

Dry ice consists of solid _____.

Carbon dioxide

Put these cities in order from west to east: San Francisco, Reno, Los Angeles.

Ⓐ **San Francisco, Reno, Los Angeles**

When was the California gold rush?

Ⓒ **1849**

A child is holding a box of coins that contains the same number of pennies, nickels, dimes, quarters, half dollars and silver dollars. If the value of the money in the box is $22.92, how many quarters are in the box?

12 quarters

The number of each coin is n. The value in cents: pennies: n   nickels: 5n

dimes: 10n   quarters: 25n   half dollars: 50n   silver dollars: 100n

Add the values: 191n = 2292   n = 12

The space shuttle travels about _____ times faster than a bullet.

Ⓒ **20 times faster**

A bullet travels approximately 700 - 1500 mph

The space shuttle's speed is approximately 17,500 mph

ANSWERS

ANSWERS

Challenge 81

When 36 gallons are poured into an empty tank,
it will be 3/4 full. How many gallons does the tank hold?

48 gallons

If 36 gallons are 3/4 of the tank, then each 1/4 is 12.

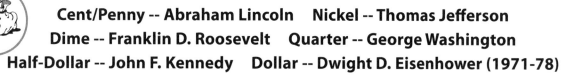

Six presidents are portrayed on U.S. coins. Name five.

Cent/Penny -- Abraham Lincoln   Nickel -- Thomas Jefferson
Dime -- Franklin D. Roosevelt   Quarter -- George Washington
Half-Dollar -- John F. Kennedy   Dollar -- Dwight D. Eisenhower (1971-78)

Answer two of these facts about rocks and minerals.

The hardest natural substance found on earth is: Diamond
The most common rock in the earth's crust: Basalt
What type of rock forms when magma cools and solidifies? Igneous

How many time zones are in the continental United States?

4 time zones

What is the name of the Prime Minister of India who was
assassinated on October 31, 1984?

Indira Gandhi

Eric is half his father's height. Eric's pet dog is half Eric's height and also twice
the height of Eric's pet cat. Eric's hamster is 1/4 the height of the cat.
If Eric's and the hamster's height total 34 inches, how tall is Eric?

32 inches

Hamster: n Cat: $4n$ Dog: $8n$ Eric: $16n$ Dad: $32n$
$n + 16n = 34$ $n = 2$

Baseball teams often "retire" numbers when a star player ends his career.
For example, 9 teams have retired the number "5". This means that
no other player will ever wear that number for that team.
Of the first 50 numbers,
how many numbers have been "retired" by at least one team?

 46 out of 50

46 out of 50   Only 28, 38, 46 and 48 have not been retired by any team.

ANSWERS

ANSWERS

Challenge 82

The largest gold nugget was found at Moliagul, Victoria, Australia in 1869 and weighed approximately 156 pounds.
What size cube is closest to the volume of 156 pounds of gold?

Ⓐ **6 inch cube**

Name the person portrayed on each denomination of U.S. paper currency:

**$1: Washington $2: Jefferson $5: Lincoln $10: Hamilton
$20: Jackson $50: Grant $100: Franklin**

Dry ice is extremely cold. Its temperature is:

Ⓑ **-109° F**

Niagara Falls drains one of the Great Lakes into another Great Lake.
Name the two Great Lakes.

Niagara Falls drains Lake Erie into Lake Ontario.

When did the first spacecraft land on Mars?

Ⓒ **1971**

If there are n shoes in a closet,
how many pairs of shoes are in the closet?

.5n

2 shoes per pair

How far above the earth did the space shuttle orbit?

Ⓐ **200-385 miles**

ANSWERS

ANSWERS

Challenge 83

Put the following numbers in order from smallest to largest.

.0899462
.0997
.10001

Stan bought a car for *n* dollars and paid $1750 in sales tax.
Mark lives in a different state where the sales tax is 1% lower.
He paid the same amount for the car as Stan (*n* dollars) and then
paid sales tax of $1500. What was the price of the car before sales tax?

$25,000

The difference of 1% was $1750 - $1500 = $250
If 1% of n is $250, then n must be $25,000

Granite is a type of:

Ⓐ **Igneous Rock**

Name four of the five most populous countries in Europe.
(Include Russia in Europe)

1) Russia 142 million   **2) Germany 82 million**
3) France 63 million   **4) Britain 62 million**
5) Italy 60 million

How many years was the Unites States involved in the Vietnam War?

Ⓓ **20**

Flash ran *n* yards in 3 seconds.
How many inches did he run?

36*n*

36 inches in a yard

Geostationary satellites move in sync with the earth's orbit.
How high do they orbit?

Ⓒ **22,400 miles**

ANSWERS

ANSWERS

Challenge 84

How many different arrangements are possible with five pictures and five hooks?

120

(5 x 4 x 3 x 2 x 1 = 120)

A television that normally sells for $400 is on sale for 20% off. What is the total price for the television if the sales tax rate is 5%?

$336

20% off = $320   Sales tax: 5% of $320 = $16 $320 + $16 = $336

One of the animals below has roughly the same ratio of brain weight to body weight as a human.

Ⓑ **Mouse (1/40)**

How large is the largest land animal in the Antarctic?

Ⓓ **1/2 inch long**

A wingless midge which is less than 1/2 inch long.

Name four of the five United State's presidents who were in office during the Vietnam War.

Eisenhower, Kennedy, Johnson, Nixon, Ford

If Flash runs at a pace of *n* feet per second, how many miles will he run in an hour?

$$\frac{15n}{22} \text{ miles per hour}$$

n feet per second means that Flash can go 3600n feet in an hour because there are 3600 seconds in an hour.

3600n feet in an hour means that Flash can go $\frac{3600n}{5280}$ miles in an hour because there are 5280 feet in a mile. 3600 ÷ 5280 = 15/22

The space shuttle's large external tank is loaded with more than _____ gallons of super-cold liquid oxygen and liquid hydrogen.

Ⓒ **500,000**

ANSWERS

ANSWERS

Challenge 85

A cube has a volume of 64 cubic feet.
What is the length of each of its sides?

4 feet

Volume = side x side x side   4 x 4 x 4 = 64 cubic feet

What is the percent of increase if a salary is increased from $60,000 to $75,000?

25%

Percent of increase is change divided by the original salary:
$15,000 ÷ $60,000 = .25 or 25%

What percent of the motor cortex in the human brain
(the part of the brain which controls all movement in the body)
is devoted to the muscles of the hands?

Ⓓ **25%**

What is the approximate population of Australia?

Ⓐ **23,000,000**

How long after General Lee surrendered was Lincoln assassinated?

Ⓐ **5 days**

What is the sum of three consecutive multiples of
5 if the smallest number is *n*?

3*n* + 15

Smallest: *n*   Next: *n* + 5   Next: *n* + 10

How fast did the space shuttle travel?

Ⓒ **17,500 mph**

ANSWERS

ANSWERS

Challenge 86

Three pieces of pie are eaten as shown.
What fraction of the pie is left?

1/20

1/5 + 1/4 + 1/2 = 19/20

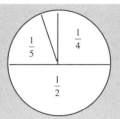

What is the percent of decrease if a
salary is decreased from $75,000 to $60,000?

20%

Percent of decrease is change divided by the original salary:
$15,000 ÷ $75,000 = .20 or 20%

The colors of visible light are:
Red, Yellow, Blue, Violet, Orange, Green, Indigo
Which one has the longest wavelength and which one has the shortest?

Longest: Red   Shortest: Violet

Luke is living in Kuwait. His mom, who lives in Chicago, wants to call him.
Luke gets up at 5:00 A.M. and goes to bed at 7:00 P.M. Kuwait time.
What would be a good time for Luke's mom to call him (Chicago time)?

Ⓓ **10:00 P.M.**

Kuwait is 9 hours ahead of Chicago. Luke is awake from 8:00 P.M. to 10:00 A.M. Chicago time.

How long after the Confederate defeat at Gettysburg did the Civil War end?

Ⓓ **Approximately two years**

Alicia's salary is $5000 more than 1/4 of Dan's salary.
If Dan's salary is *n*, what is Alicia's salary?

.25*n* + $5000

How old was the youngest soldier to serve in the Civil War?

Ⓐ **8 years old**

ANSWERS

ANSWERS

Challenge 87

Laura will roll one die two times. If she rolls a three with any roll, she wins $1,000,000. What is her probability of winning the $1,000,000?

Ⓐ 11/36

*The only way Laura will lose is if she doesn't roll a "3" on the two rolls.
The probability of not getting a "3" each roll is 5/6.
5/6 x 5/6 = 25/36   The probability of getting at least one "3" is $1 - \frac{25}{36} = \frac{11}{36}$*

A car uses one gallon of gas to travel 35 miles.
If gas cost $4 per gallon, what will it cost to take a 700 mile trip?

$80

700 miles ÷ 35 mpg = 20 gallons x $4 per gallon = $80

The use of chlorofluorocarbons (CFC's) has been phased out because of their ability to destroy the ozone layer. The destructive power of CFC's is illustrated by the fact that one chlorine atom can destroy up to _____ molecules of ozone.

Ⓑ 100,000

What percent of the corn grown in the United States goes to the production of ethanol? (2011)

Ⓓ 40%

How many voyages to the New World did Columbus make?

Four

If a flea can jump *n* centimeters high, how many meters can it jump?

.01*n* meters

There are 100 centimeters in a meter

Put the following in order from shortest to tallest:

**Statue of Liberty: 305 feet
Tallest redwood in California: 389 feet
Great Pyramid near Cairo: 481 feet
Washington Monument: 555 feet**

ANSWERS

ANSWERS

Challenge 88

The length of a marathon is 26.2 miles. If a runner traveled at a pace of 6 mph, how many minutes would it take him/her to finish a marathon?

262 minutes

(If the speed was 60 mph, the runner would travel a mile per minute and finish in 26.2 minutes. 6 mph is 10 times slower ----262 minutes.

If 3 ounces of dark chocolate cost $1.50, what does a pound of dark chocolate cost?

$8

50 cents an ounce x 16 ounces in a pound = $8

The boiling point of water is 212°F and the freezing point of water is 32°F. What is the boiling and freezing point of water in the Celsius scale?

100° C and 0° C

The wettest place in the United States is Mt. Waialeale in Hawaii. It averages _____ inches of rain each year.

Ⓑ **400**

Magellan started his journey around the world in 1519 with five ships and 265 sailors. By the time the trip was done in 1522, how many ships and sailors returned home?

Ⓓ **1 ship and 18 sailors**

If a kangaroo can jump *n* meters, how many millimeters can it jump?

1000*n*

1000 millimeters in a meter

One silkworm's cocoon, when unfolded, can have a piece of silk _____ feet long.

Ⓒ **3000 feet**

ANSWERS

ANSWERS

Challenge 89

If a person who is 6 feet tall has a shadow of 4 feet, how tall is a tree that casts a shadow of 24 feet?

36 feet

$\dfrac{6}{4} = \dfrac{n}{24}$ $4n = 144$ $n = 36$

If milk cost $6.40 per gallon, what does a cup of milk cost?

40 cents

$6.40 ÷ 16 cups in a gallon = 40 cents

The Kelvin scale starts with a "0" at absolute zero.
What is the boiling and freezing point of water in the Kelvin scale?

Ⓐ **373.15 K and 273.15 K**

The definition of a desert is:
"A location that gets less than _____ of rain per year."

Ⓓ **10 inches**

According to the U.S. Department of Agriculture, ___ of all land in the United States is owned by the Federal government.

Ⓒ **29%**

If you know your weight in pounds, you can find your mass by dividing by 32: mass = weight / 32
If you know your mass, how do you find your weight?

weight = mass x 32

$$mass = \dfrac{weight}{32}$$

Multiply both sides by 32   weight = mass x 32

How long do fingernails grow in a year?

Ⓒ **1.5 inches**

ANSWERS

ANSWERS

Challenge 90

A meter is a little longer than a yard. A centimeter is equal to:

Ⓒ **A little less than 1/2 inch**

(.39 inches)

What does it cost to keep a 100-watt bulb on for 24 hours when electricity cost 10 cents per kilowatt hour?

24 cents

100 watts is 1/10 of a kilowatt, therefore the cost is one cent per hour.

An average person at sea level has about 13-14 kilopascals (kPa) of oxygen in their bloodstream. University College of London medical researcher Dan Martin and three colleagues climbed Mount Everest and measured their own blood oxygen level near the summit. What happened to their oxygen level?

Ⓒ **Lowest ever measured in live people**

(Their oxygen level was between 2.5 and 4 kPa.)

The largest desert in the world is:

Ⓐ **Sahara**

Who becomes president if both the president and vice-president die?

Speaker of the House

Next in line are the following: President pro tempore of the Senate, Secretary of State, Secretary of the Treasury, Secretary of Defense, Attorney General, Secretary of the Interior, Secretary of Agriculture, Secretary of Commerce

A car rental company charges $45 per day plus 11 cents per mile. If a car was rented for d days and driven m miles, what was the cost of the rental in dollars?

$45d + \$.11m$ = cost in dollars

What percent of the world's population was on Facebook in 2012?

Ⓑ **15%**

ANSWERS

ANSWERS

Challenge 91

Convert the following base 5 decimal into a base 10 fraction: .4

Ⓑ **4/5**

.4 in base 10 is 4/10   .4 in base 5 is 4/5

If $960 will last 12 days for 3 people,
how long will it last if there are 4 people?

9 days

If $960 will last 12 days for 3 people, then it will last 3 x 12 = 36 days for one person.
2 people: 36 ÷ 2 = 18   4 people 36 ÷ 4 = 9

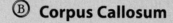

The neural bridge that connects the two hemispheres to each other and
is centrally located in the brain is called the:

Ⓑ **Corpus Callosum**

What is the average ocean temperature?

Ⓐ **39°F**

How much tea was ruined during the Boston Tea Party?

Ⓒ **90,000 pounds**

Juan is paid $22.50 per hour and a bonus of $75 each week.
If Juan was paid $862.50 one week, how many hours did he work?

35 hours

22.5n + 75 = 862.50   22.5n = 787.50   n = 35

What is the heaviest fruit?

Pumpkin

ANSWERS

ANSWERS

Challenge 92

What is the probability of winning a 6 number lottery where the numbers range from 1-40?

Ⓒ **1/3,838,380**

1st pick: 6/40 chance of your number, 2nd pick: 5/39 chance of your number, 3rd pick: 4/38 chance of your number, 4th pick: 3/37 chance of your number, 5th pick 2/36 chance of your number, 6th pick: 1/35 chance of your number.
6/40 x 5/39 x 4/38 x 3/37 x 2/36 x 1/35 = 1/3,838,380

A friend offered to pay .50% of your $1500 dental bill. How much of the $1500 will be left after your friend's contribution?

$1492.50

.50% is $\frac{1}{2}$ %   1% of $1500 = $15 $\frac{1}{2}$ % of $1500 = $7.50

Newborn human babies are typically 1/20 of the weight of the mother. What fraction of the mother's weight is a newborn kangaroo?

Ⓓ **1/50,000**

Kangaroos weigh between 1 and 2 grams when they are born.
The tiny baby, called a joey, climbs up its mother's belly and into her pouch.
An adult kangaroo weighs approximately 75 kilograms or 75,000 grams.

What is the population of the world's least populated country?

Ⓑ **800**

Who wrote the pamphlet "Common Sense"?

Ⓑ **Thomas Paine**

A barn contains cows, ducks, and a three-legged dog named Tripod. There are 5 times as many cows as ducks and a total of 333 legs. How many ducks are in the barn?

15 ducks

Ducks: n   Duck legs: 2n   Cows: 5n   Cow legs: 20n
Equation: 22n + 3 (Tripod) = 333   22n = 330   n = 15

What were Aristotle's four elements?

Water, earth, air, and fire

ANSWERS

ANSWERS

Challenge 93

A science book incorrectly stated that the speed of light was approximately 300,000 miles per second. What is the most likely explanation for this mistake?

**They meant to put the speed in kilometers per second.
The formula to change miles into kilometers is: 1 mile = 1.61 kilometers**

The speed of light is 186,200 miles per second
186,200 x 1.61 = 299,782 kilometers per second

In 2010, Trevor's $100,000 salary was increased by 200%. In 2011, Trevor's salary was decreased by 100%. What is his salary now?

$0

$100,000 increased by 200% is $300,000 $300,000 decreased by 100% is $0

A blood pressure reading of 160/110 is:

Ⓓ **Extremely high**

How many Alaskas will fit into the lower 48 states?

Ⓓ **5**

Who wrote the first draft of The Declaration of Independence?

Thomas Jefferson

When each side of a square is tripled, the area increases by 392 square inches. What is the area of the original square?

49 inches

Original square side: n Area: n^2
Side triples: $3n$ Area: $9n^2$
Equation: $9n^2 - n^2 = 392$ $8n^2 = 392$ $n^2 = 49$

Very large waves are called tsunamis. They can move at speeds as high as:

Ⓒ **500 miles per hour**

ANSWERS

ANSWERS

Challenge 94

If the weight of a dozen donuts is 3 pounds,
how many ounces does one donut weigh?

4 ounces

3 pounds are 48 ounces   48 ounces ÷ 12 = 4 ounces

If you spend $15 per day for cigarettes,
what will your total cost for cigarettes be if you smoke for 10 years?
(365 days in a year)

$54,750

365 days x 10 years x $15 = $54,750

On a summer afternoon, a car is traveling at a speed of 60 miles per hour. A ball is hanging inside the car as shown below. The driver slams on the brakes and skids to a stop to avoid a deer in the road. What happens to the hanging ball when the brakes are applied forcefully?

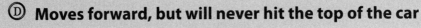

Ⓓ **Moves forward, but will never hit the top of the car**

How many miles is Hawaii from California?

Ⓓ **2,390 miles**

What was George Washington's annual salary while he was president?

Ⓓ **$25,000**

In the year 2000, Larry is twice as old as Curly. Ten years later, their ages add up to 53. How old was Larry in the year 2000?

22 years old

Year 2000:   Curly: n   Larry: 2n
10 years later: Curly n + 10   Larry: 2n + 10
Equation: 3n + 20 = 53   3n = 33   n = 11

There are currently (2012) five official dwarf planets. Name two.

Pluto, Ceres, Haumea, Eris, and Makemake.

ANSWERS

ANSWERS

Challenge 95

Stanley found a bag of money. He gave 1/2 to charity, 1/4 to his sister and 1/8 to his brother. Stanley now has $10 remaining. How much money was in the bag when he found it?

$80

He has 1/8 remaining, which is equal to $10 1/8 of $80 = $10

Four children inherited money from their parents. The oldest child received half the money while the second oldest received half of what was left. The youngest two then split the remaining money. If the youngest two each received $50,000, what was the total amount of money the four children inherited?

$400,000

Youngest: $50,000 + $50,000   Next oldest: $100,000   Next oldest: $200,000

Which of the following is an optimal blood pressure?

Ⓒ **115/75**

The Arctic and Antarctic circles are closest to which of the following lines of latitude?

Ⓑ **67**

In what year was the Louisiana Purchase?

Ⓒ **1803**

A store determined that in a year's time .1% of its checks were bad. If the store had 5 bad checks in a year's time, how many total checks did it receive during the year?

5000 checks

.1% = .001   .001 of the checks or .001n = 5   n = 5 ÷ .001 or 5000

At the top of Pikes Peak, the oxygen in the air is _____ percent lower than at sea level.

Ⓒ **40%**

ANSWERS

Challenge 96

A movie starts at 7:30 and goes until 10:00.
At what time is the movie 1/3 over?

8:20

Movie is 2.5 hours or 150 minutes. 1/3 is 50 minutes 7:30 + 50 minutes = 8:20

A person with a net worth of $1000 gave $50 to charity.
How much should a person with a net worth of 10 billion dollars
give to charity to give the same proportional amount?

$500,000,000

50 is 1/20 of 1000   1/20 of 10 billion is 500 million

The following sentence appeared in a science magazine: "While liquid hydrogen is the densest form of the fuel, keeping it at the required 480 degrees below zero in the on-board storage tank is expensive and difficult."

What mistake did the author make?

480 degrees below zero is lower than absolute zero.

The Tropics of Cancer and Capricorn lie parallel
to the equator at about _____ latitude.

Ⓑ 23°

The Louisiana Purchase increased the size of the United States by:

Ⓓ 100%

If I add the page number of the book I am reading to the 3 previous pages,
I get the number 374. What page am I reading?

Page 95

Page reading: n Previous page: $n - 1$ Previous page: $n - 2$
Previous page: $n - 3$ Equation: $4n - 6 = 374$ $4n = 380$ $n = 95$

The average temperature at 40,000 feet is approximately:

Ⓐ -60° F

ANSWERS

ANSWERS
Challenge 97

1/4 pound of gold is going to be shared by 4 people.
How many ounces will each receive?

One ounce

1/4 pound is 4 ounces

The charge to ride a taxi is a $5 flat fee plus $1.25 per mile plus a 20% tip.
What would you pay for a 20 mile taxi ride?

$36

$5 + (20 x $1.25) = $30   20% of $30 = $6

The headline in a newspaper read: *"Flu vaccines are only 59% effective."*
Which of the following sentences
best explains the meaning of the headline?

Ⓒ **If you get the vaccine every year for the rest of your life,
you will get the flu, on average, only 2 times for every 5 times an
unvaccinated person gets the flu.**

In which continent is Buddhism a major religion?

Ⓓ **Asia**

The United States paid France _____ per acre for all the land
they acquired with the Louisiana Purchase.

Ⓑ **3 cents**

828,000 square miles x 640 acres per square mile = 529,920,000 acres.
Cost was $15,000,000 divided by 529,920,000 acres = 2.8 cents per acre.

If you multiply a certain number by 5, your answer is
the same as when you add 144 to the number. What is the number?

The number is 36

$5n = n + 144$ $4n = 144$ $n = 36$

As the altitude increases, the oxygen content of the air
decreases dramatically. At 20,000 feet there is what fraction of
the oxygen in the air when compared to sea level?

Ⓑ **1/2**

ANSWERS

Challenge 98

A house that is 18 feet tall has a shadow of 3 feet.
If Dave has a shadow of 10 inches, how many feet tall is Dave?

5 feet

18 feet/3 feet = n inches/10 inches   3n = 180   n = 60 inches

A rent-to-own plan for a television requires a $75 monthly payment for two years. If the television was paid for with cash, it would cost $500. How much more money will a person pay using a rent-to-own plan compared to paying with cash?

$1300

$75 x 24 months = $1800 $1800 - $500 = $1300

The atmosphere is divided into four main sections. The troposphere is the lowest and has a typical temperature of 68° F. The next highest level is the stratosphere with a typical temperature of -60° F. The next is the mesosphere with a typical temperature of -90° F. The highest section of the atmosphere is the thermosphere. What is a typical temperature in the thermosphere?

Ⓓ **1000° to 2000° F**

Even though the temperature is high, because it is so near a vacuum, there is not enough contact with the small number of atoms of gas to transfer much heat. Therefore, one would not feel warm in the thermosphere.

There are five Great Lakes --- name four.
Erie, Ontario, Superior, Huron, Michigan

The following is at the very end of the _____ "that this nation under God shall have a new birth of freedom; and that government of the people, by the people, for the people, shall not perish from the earth."

Ⓑ **Gettysburg Address**

A bookstore owner buys a book for half off the retail price (*n*) and then sells it for 20% more than she bought it for. What does the bookstore owner sell the book for?

.6n

Half off retail price: .5n   + 20% of .5n   .2 x .5n = .1n   .5n +.1n = .6n

Compare the weight of your skin to the weight of your brain.
Ⓒ **Skin weighs three times as much**

ANSWERS

ANSWERS

Challenge 99

Objects that are dropped from a tall building or an airplane increase their speed as they fall. If you ignore the effect of air slowing the object down, by how much does the speed of the object increase each second?

Ⓑ 22 mph

The speed increases by 32 feet per second each second the object falls. Let's figure what that increase in speed is in miles per hour each second: 32 feet per second x 3600 seconds in an hour = 115,200 feet per hour. 115,200 feet per hour ÷ 5280 feet in a mile = 21.8 miles per hour for each second of free fall.

A clerk at a bookstore wants to sell six books and average $20 per book sale. She sold five books at the following prices: $18, $18, $18, $16, $14. What must she sell the sixth book for to average $20 per book?

$36

The quick way to solve this problem is to see how far away from $20 each sale was: -$2, -$2, -$2, -$4, -$6 The total is negative 16 so she must sell the last book for $16 more than $20, which is $36.

A barometric pressure of 27.05 is:

Ⓑ Associated with category 5 hurricanes

Name the four time zones in the continental United States.

Eastern, Central, Mountain, Pacific

"Four score and seven years ago" is the beginning of the Gettysburg Address. How many years is "Four score and seven years"?

Ⓒ 87

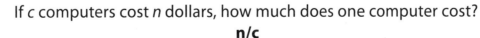

If c computers cost n dollars, how much does one computer cost?

n/c

If two computers cost $10, then one would cost $5.
10 ÷ 2 = 5
Divide the dollars by the number of computers: n ÷ c

In the formula $E=mc^2$, the E stands for energy. What does the m and the c stand for?

m: mass c: the speed of light

ANSWERS

ANSWERS

Challenge 100

A flea 1/16th of an inch tall can jump 10 inches high.
If a cat that is one foot tall could jump like a flea,
how high could it jump?

160 feet high

A flea can jump 160 times its height.

What is the cost of carpet for a room that is
10 yards by 8 yards if the cost of carpet is $2 per square foot?

$1440

30 feet x 24 feet = 720 square feet   720 x $2 = $1440

Winds can make cold temperatures feel even colder.
Wind chill charts tell how cold it feels based on
temperature and wind speed. If the temperature is 10° F and
the wind speed is 40 mph, what is the wind chill?

Ⓓ **-37° F**

The lowest mountain in the world is Mount Wycheproof (Australia) which has a
summit _____ feet above the surrounding plains.

Ⓑ **140 feet**

Abraham Lincoln had _____ year/years of formal schooling.

Ⓐ **Less than one**

What is the mean of 5 consecutive multiples of 5 when the smallest is *n*?

n + 10

Smallest: n   Next: n + 5   Next: n + 10   Next: n + 15   Next: n + 20

$$\frac{5n + 50}{5} = \frac{5(n+10)}{5} = n + 10$$

How many milligrams are in a kilogram?

Ⓓ **1,000,000**

There are 1000 milligrams in a gram and 1000 grams in a kilogram.

ANSWERS

Notes

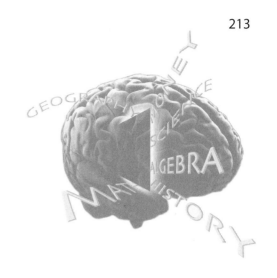

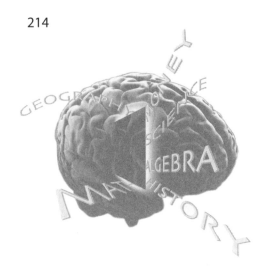

Notes

Notes

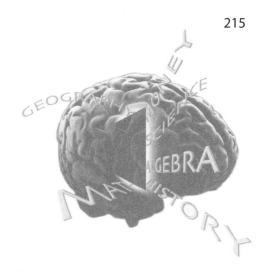

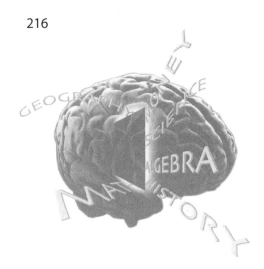

Notes

Notes

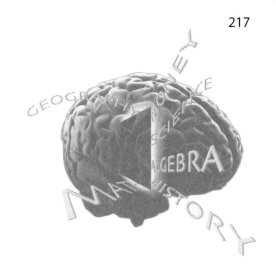

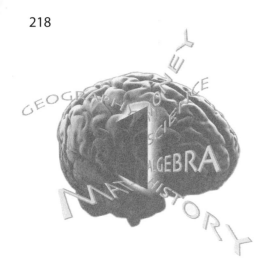

Notes

Notes

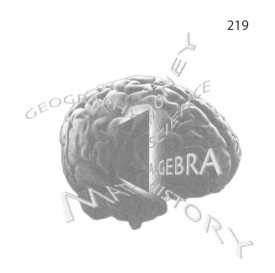

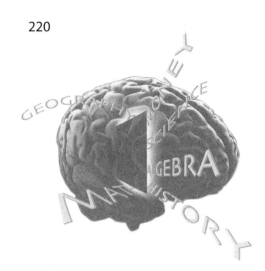

Notes

Notes

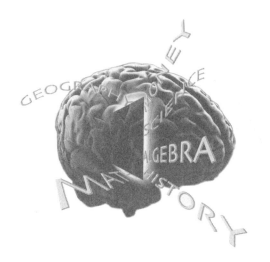

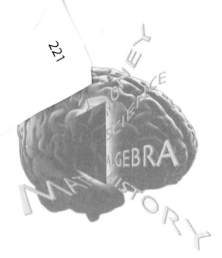

Notes

Notes

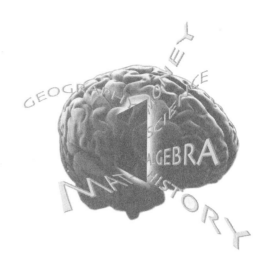

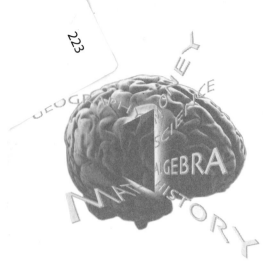

Notes